Sew Crazy

with

DECORATIVE THREADS & STITCHES

ALICE KOLB

American Quilter's Society

P. O. Box 3290 • Paducah, KY 42002-3290
FAX: 270-898-1173 *www.AQSquilt.com*

Located in Paducah, Kentucky, the American Quilter's Society (AQS) is dedicated to promoting the accomplishments of today's quilters. Through its publications and events, AQS strives to honor today's quiltmakers and their work and to inspire future creativity and innovation in quiltmaking.

EDITOR: BARBARA SMITH
GRAPHIC DESIGN: ELAINE WILSON
COVER DESIGN: MICHAEL BUCKINGHAM
PHOTOGRAPHY: CHARLES R. LYNCH

Library of Congress Cataloging-in-Publication Data
Kolb, Alice.
    Sew crazy with decorative threads and stitches / by Alice Allen Kolb.
    p. cm.
    ISBN 1-57432-783-6
    1. Embroidery, Machine. 2. Crazy quilt. 3. Patchwork. I. Title.
    TT772 .K65 2001
      746.44'028--dc21

                  2001005684

Additional copies of this book may be ordered from the American Quilter's Society, PO Box 3290, Paducah, KY 42002-3290, or online at www.AQSquilt.com.

Dedication

To all stitchers whose fondness of
the crazy quilt is as dear as mine,
To students who carry my ambitious light
with their creativity, energy and skill,
To George and Alisa who walk with me
in love, hard work and loyalty,
And, to all my family and friends who cheer me on,
and stand by, to let me meet one more deadline.

Acknowledgments

My thanks to the students, co-teachers, editors, and business people who have encouraged me along the way. I am especially appreciative of Mary Honeycutt, Shirley Watkins, JoAnn Pugh-Gannon, Marty Bowne, Mary Lou Schwinn, Lorraine Torrence, Judy Simmons, Jane Garrison, Ann Henderson, and Peter and David Mancusco.

I am also grateful to Mom and Dad for believing in me and providing an education and a sense of life direction. I am grateful to my kindred creative spirit and sister, Fran; to my husband, George, for his support and patient love (and his lunches!); and to my thoughtful and encouraging daughter, Alisa. And in this latest project, I'm thankful to Barbara Smith, my editor, for encouraging me to write this book and to Sylvia Showers for her assistance in thought and samples and for her wonderful sense of humor. Thank you also to my dear Kerrville-Fredricksburg friends and the Vail girls. Opportunities became realities because of these creative people and their belief in me. I also want to thank Bernina of America, Inc.; Pfaff American Sales Corporation; and Creations of Kerrville, Texas, for loaning me sewing machines.

Contents

Introduction

Stitching embellishment is nothing new to me. I have stretched the decorative stitch potential for years, but for me, and I imagine many of you, there is still an opportunity for further artistic expression. The crazy-patch path took me one step further. The marriage of old (crazy patch) and new (sewing machine technology) stretched my machine and quilt familiarity and introduced me to an exciting art form. Now, years later, I share my approach with you. In turn, I trust you will find freedom in an age-old craft with a new twist. I hope you are driven with an excited sense of pursuit—to try stitching your way.

In the pages to follow are the specifics for sewing machine techniques. The machine is the classic tool, le crème de la crème, used effortlessly to enhance quilt blocks. Each chapter is written as a classroom lesson. My years of teaching have always been based on "what would I like to know?" and "what questions do I hear?" By approaching the segments of machine technique this way, hopefully you can easily find the information you are seeking and apply it to your project.

Chapter 1 summarizes the excellent resources that communicate the history of crazy quilts. Technical instruction keeps us from going tech crazy, so Chapter 2 addresses the sewing machine and related tools from both a practical and a creative perspective. Chapter 3 explores the practical transition from idea to project. Because beginnings are at various places for each of us, different starting places are explored. Hopefully, you will find a beginning that is right for you. Chapter 4 is a condensed textile reference designed as a shopping checklist, a guide to get you on your way. Chapter 5 introduces you to thread types and stabilizers. Questions regarding "which needle to which thread," and tension adjustments are discussed in user-friendly language. Chapter 6 will show you how to appliqué, from pinning to stitching, in a method I call "straight-stitch appliqué." Chapter 7 explores the various stitches and stitch combos, and tips on sewing decorative stitches on patches. In Chapter 8, you will find hints on sewing borders and the technique of tying a quilt, along with bindings and signature labels. And last, but not least, Chapter 9 focuses on projects. I've covered my favorites with suggestions for adding your own to the list.

As you read through the book, remember you are limited only by your imagination. Notice the relationship of today and yesterday in stitches, in fabric, and in style. It has been said, and I agree, that duplication challenged by innovation must be the supreme compliment to the masters of old. Then our new approach to machine stitching must surely be just that.

Chapter 1

Crazy-Patch History

History might be defined as an account of the way things were done or events have happened. Although past, history always affects the present. There is always a connection between the two. We connect the past with today when we admire an old house, an old community, or our special interest, old quilts. Reflecting on the patterns, fabrics, and stitches of yesterday, we naturally want to know how they were done, while we concern ourselves with the creative possibilities of today. Perhaps it is this puzzle that pushes us into the history of the early quiltmaking style called crazy patch or crazy quilt.

Basically, the historic crazy quilt (era 1875–1900) was a random arrangement of fancy colored fabrics sewn to a solid foundation fabric. The sewn patches were then embellished, in embroidery stitches from humble to lavish, and sewn along the seam edges, while the patch interiors were often decorated with a variety of embroidered or painted pictures. Ribbons, lace, beads, and collected trinkets were added as the quiltmaker saw fit.

1876 Centennial Exposition

The last quarter of the nineteenth century saw the crazy quilt rise to its height of popularity, with many historians crediting the Japanese exhibits in the 1876 Centennial Exposition in Philadelphia for much of its charm. Record crowds from far and wide found the Japanese show breathtaking. Most popular among the countless displays was a large exhibit of Japanese artifacts and screens featuring tessellation and puzzle-type designs.

While the Centennial Japanese puzzle exhibits were at their height of popularity, the many women's magazine editors were also hard at work featuring crazy patch in almost every publication. They were constantly making an effort to upstage one another, printing varied articles on ways to stitch and embellish crazy quilts. Features of beautiful motif patterns and "new" ideas, such as the fan and other pieced shapes, complemented the trends in decorating and soon were at every woman's disposal. *Harper's Bazaar* magazine even took the position, "We have discarded in our modern quilts the regular geometric design once so popular, and substituted what are more like the changing figures of the kaleidoscope, or the beauty and infinite variety of oriental mosaics" (*The American Quilt Story*, Rodale Press, 1991). Another popular publication named *Diagrams of Quilt, Sofa and Pincushion Patterns*, printed by the Ladies Art Company in 1894, provided patterns and yard goods by mail from such sources as Montgomery Wards and Sears, Roebuck and Company. There seemed to be a kindred spirit among the exhibits, the popular magazines, and the modern woman's needlework.

In retrospect, it is difficult to imagine whether enthusiasm about the crazy quilt evolved primarily from the exhibits of the mosaic imagery in the Japanese halls or from the promotion of mass-media women's magazines like *The Household, Godey's,* and *Home Companion.* Who can really say? But one thing is for sure, there was a widespread enthusiasm that created the fad of sewing quilts with irregular fabric shapes and embellishing them "to the nines."

The Centennial and the women's magazines seemed to fit together hand in glove. In addition to the hoopla about the artistic expositions, the Centennial also marked a significant change in the quilter's choices of fabrics and supplies. Familiar block-printed fabrics were rapidly becoming scarce as the mass production of roller-printed fabrics forced their prominence in the market. At the same time, silk production in the United States was increasing like wildfire, and silk prices were falling rapidly. American mills were producing silk in massive amounts, and by the late 1880s, the United States was manufacturing much of the world's silk. The crazy-quilt fad intensified so much that scrap madness set in. Fabric scraps, silk in particular, became so popular that monies and ribbons were offered in numerous contests, and scrap-patch bundles were advertised in popular magazines. Although the fancy-work craze usually resulted in quilts, equally popular was everything from pillows to evening slippers.

Crazy-Patch Resourcefulness

From these scrap-madness beginnings arose a second side of the industry's fad—decorative stitch patterns. Embroidery patterns, both printed and perforated, were available in magazines, then traded among friends and neighbors, church circles, and quilting bees. Simply styled embroidery motifs sewn in the center of crazy patches became popular about 1880. Women transferred motif designs from magazines, then stitched the shapes in chain and stem outline embroidery. Patterns often included flowers, small children, Oriental designs like cattails and fans, and of course, religious symbols. Most crazy-quilt makers considered the outline embroidery patterns to be essential to their crazy patch. Other women painted their fabrics, then added ribbon and trim.

The popular fad produced an endless variety of crazy-quilt supplies, assortments of silks from the strong silk industry, perforated designs for embroidery, and the latest gadgetry for design transfer. In addition, the nineteenth-century stitcher had the resourcefulness from her heritage, that is, the skill to recycle fabrics from ties, vests, dresses, and other garments. Regardless of the crazy-patch approach, each woman styled her "crazy" in a personal way while bonding to the commonly held theme of lavish fabrics embroidered and embellished, merely for the sake of beauty. *(continued)*

Influenced by the beautiful Japanese mosaic designs, the bits and pieces concept brought out another quality of the modern nineteenth-century stitcher. Again and again, the attitude of the crazy quilt touched her moral discipline, the philosophy of bridling leisure time. "Waste not, want not" was a common denominator, and sewing "a thing of beauty from nothing" reinforced a strength of self-control, of idle time spent advantageously. In addition, this style of needlework supported her self-imposed discipline of perfection and neatness.

The Victorian woman wanted her home to reflect not only attractive adornment but also peace, a shelter from the outside world. When she showed her crazy quilt in her finest room, she communicated her personal philosophy and her desire to create a beautiful family sanctuary. The late nineteenth-century woman was also contemplating her heritage. She typically wanted to be modern but maintained the desire to hold on to her ethics. She felt conflict in fashion, in the modernization of technology, and decreed that what was old might be considered new.

The news media and society picked up the spontaneous attitude of the crazy quilt. The fad grew so popular that a magazine even printed a party idea for a "crazy day." Lamps were to be placed on sofas so the guests would sit on the floor, and the party menu featured an odd combination of foods, such as pickle relish on cake, merely for the "crazy" notion of it all. People tagged along, and the crazy quilt and its endless varieties became almost every woman's favorite. Newspapers and magazines quoted neighborly jokes, such as "the end result of your work will surely be crazy" and "don't become crazy to finish it." The fad was hot. Everyone seemed wrapped up in the stitches of crazy patch.

Fabrics and Patterns

Traditionally, the quilts were cut from scrap pieces, sewn by hand onto a muslin base, then hand embellished. The stitcher placed a colored odd-shaped patch of silk, cotton, or other fabric on a foundation fabric, then added a second patch atop the first, placing them right sides together. She stitched one seam, then flipped the second piece outward, revealing two patches. She continued until the foundation was covered.

As with today's quilts, foundation units were styled in a variety of ways. Whole cloth, with all the patch pieces sewn to one large foundation, was popular, as was the idea of working in patchwork tiles, which were multiple crazy-patch squares sewn next to each other. Solid-colored sashing strips were occasionally sewn around the blocks in a contained style, then lavishly decorated. Motifs, ranging from Kate Greenaway figures to spiders and butterflies, were collected and embroidered in the patch centers. It was popular to create embroidery designs of family homes, dogs, and cats. Political ribbons, family memorabilia, and embroidered names and dates were also used. Every quilter individualized her quilts. Occasionally, cut shapes, such as baby blocks or hexagons, were pieced then hand embroidered with a wealth of stitches collected from favorite magazines, such as *Godey's* and *Home Companion*, etc. The common theme of the crazy-quilt style was one of personalizing and embroidering—the more the better.

Although most crazy-quilt styles are grouped together, there was a difference in the styles within the 25 years of popularity. Random patching was most popular in the 1880s. From the mid nineteenth century, it was also fairly common to see all-over mosaic designs

   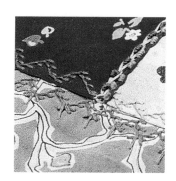

of hexagons or diamonds. The 1870s brought the Log Cabin, and the 1880s introduced fans and the string style of random piecing. From all these varieties, the random-shaped patchwork is the only style that historians consider true crazy patch. The quilts were often sentimental, both happy and sad, and a wide variety of interpretations of wedding and mourning quilts were made, commonly from the coats and dresses of such occasions.

Silk fabrics predominated in the early phases of the crazy-patch fad. Then, by the turn of the century, wool and cotton scraps became quite popular. As with all phases of this fad, opinions varied about appropriate fabric choices. In the *Lady's Handbook of Fancy and Ornamental Work*, Florence Hartley wrote, "We think the real old patchwork of bits of calico is infinitely prettier than bits of silk sewn together for parlor ornaments." Over time, finishing the quilt was simplified, perhaps even understated. Tying or tacking was commonly used to secure the patched foundation to a backing, and a simple binding finished the edge.

Regardless of the stitcher's viewpoint and the materials used, the crazy quilt easily fit in its proper place in the family room of the house, the parlor, because the quilt's fancy stitches and bits of memory fabrics gave a bit of glow to an often otherwise meager existence. For nearly a quarter of a century, the crazy quilt held its position in popular needlework, enduring both a love and hate status. In criticism, the early crazy quilt of silk and velvet was loathed and referred to as "a decorative bauble—usually more for show than warmth." In its praise, it was referred to as "a tie to the beauty we all desire."

Then, ironically, as quickly as it came, the crazy-patch style began to disappear. By 1888, magazines were pushing women to try something new, unembellished baby blocks and Log Cabins. The crazy quilt stayed, but the more simple foundation blocks infiltrated the stitcher's collection. By 1910, the crazy quilt had metamorphosed to a more modest version. Wools and cottons were commonly used, and patterns were generally more geometric. Most crazy quilts had been packed away. As with all highly popular styles, today's fad is soon gone.

To review the history of the crazy quilt is helpful. It gives us stability as we reach for new designs, fabrics, and stitches, influenced by the old. Today's crazy quilt is new, but strongly touched by the old. It's fascinating to consider the concept that what is new today is old tomorrow, and at every step of the way, "modern" is always the latest word. The crazy quilt of the 1800s was modern in its time, tied to us through history, and now our transition into a new method of construction makes it modern all over again.

Chapter 2
Equipment and Supplies

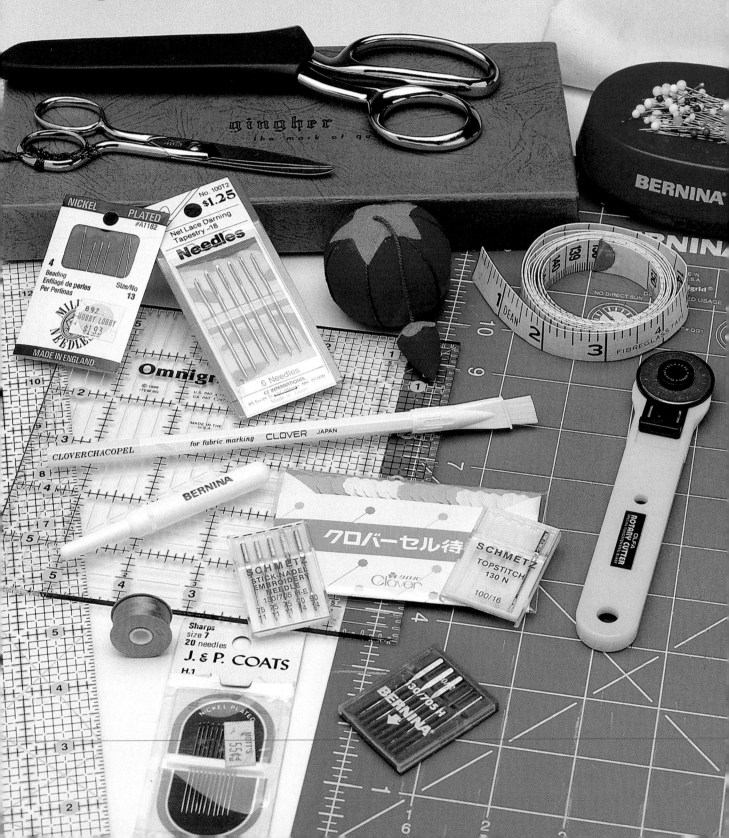

For years, I've connected to the spirit of the crazy quilt and have known I must make one. My plan for stitching was traditional. My first quilts were sewn by hand, then I thought of the possibility of using the sewing machine to do the patching and decorative embellishing stitches. The concept of machine efficiency plus unlimited stitch beauty was quite intriguing.

Then I recalled my feelings of frustration in previous attempts to sew decorative machine stitches. I remembered that the stitches sewed differently on different fabrics. I remembered, in spite of my best efforts, how the predictable length and size of each stitch row varied. Would my results be different now? What is the stitch quality when made with a modern machine? How accurate is the repetition of the stitches? Is a crazy quilt sewn by machine a feasible plan?

History of Sewing Machines

In a way, the days when a sewing machine had only a straight-stitch mechanism seem forever past, and in another way, it was just yesterday. In the early 1950s, the revolutionary addition of the zigzag stitch changed the way we could sew. For the first time in sewing-machine history, sewing was not purely functional because new machine-designed embroidery enticed the sewer to an expanded expression of creativity. From simple zigzags and scallops, half circles and ovals, the new stitches were commonly available on the post-World War II sewing machine. To sew the decorative stitches, assorted cams (small discs) were inserted into the machine then matched to a dial setting. Decorative sewing-machine possibilities were widely advertised, and the modern woman was excited. Resources, such as the 1950s era Singer Sewing how-to booklets, illustrated beautiful examples of automatic machine embroidery work, inspiring women to try the stitches "available by turning a dial." Sewing machine technology had moved beyond the basics.

However, limitations within the mechanism were a reality. After a dial-set stitch was selected, perfect fine-tuning was accomplished by adjusting the stitch length and width settings. Exact spacing was awkward to achieve because all settings were done manually, by turning one knob at a time. A slight turn too far to the left or right created different results, so it was often difficult to repeat the stitches. Also, different thicknesses of fabric created varying results. Not to be discouraged, many creative stitchers enjoyed the decorative stitch options but always fretted about the predictable inaccuracy. Every stitch row was risky.

Then, in the 1970s and 1980s, another revolutionary change occurred for the home stitcher. The computer chip appeared in a sewing machine. For the first time, the sewer

(continued on page 16)

What Do These Buttons Do?

Here is a mini-glossary of the main sewing machine knobs and dials to reassure you and answer questions. Of course, not all machines have all these features (Fig. 2–1).

Width adjustments

Many machines measure the stitch width in millimeters (¼" equals about 6 mm). Each number on the width dial is equal to 1 mm and has a width range from 0–9 mm (about ⅜"), depending on the machine. Zero indicates a straight seam – no width. The higher the number, the wider the width.

Length adjustments

Based on 6 mm equaling ¼", each number on the dial is about 1 mm. Thus a stitch length of 3 is about ⅛" long. In non-computerized machines, the stitch is measured by the inch. Short stitches are up to 20–22 stitches per inch, while the long stitches are about 6 per inch. Zero indicates no length. A setting near ½ would produce a satin stitch. The higher the number, the longer the stitch.

Reverse

The touch or knob control activates the machine to sew backward. This feature is useful for locking a stitch or defining a bar tack, which is several zigzags grouped together.

Needle-tension adjustments

The tension device is composed of two discs that contract and expand to varied degrees of tightness, con-trolling the needle thread as you sew. Most machines have a knob on the front or side with numbers ranging from 0 to 10. Generally, the middle range is a balanced tension for regular sewing. If you want more of the top thread to show, as in embroidery, select a lower tension number. If the needle thread needs to be tightened to pull up the bobbin thread, adjust the dial to a higher number. Some older machines have a plus or minus setting. Use the plus for tightening and the minus for loosening the thread.

Needle up/down

Use this feature to control the needle position when the machine stops sewing.

Needle position

The needle can be moved left and right, which is useful for positioning the edge-stitch foot or relocating the needle relative to the fabric edge.

Feed-dog position

This button or lever adjusts the feed teeth to an up (engaged) or down (disengaged) position. The feed dogs should be up for normal sewing and down for free-motion embroidery or quilting.

Presser-foot pressure

Use this knob to adjust the pressure of the foot on the fabric. Reduce pressure to prevent stretching and increase pressure for better control of sheer, slippery fabrics.

Motor speed

The speed can be varied from full to two or three reduced speed settings, which are useful when more control is needed.

Pattern begin

This is a computerized function that starts a decorative stitch at the beginning of its cycle.

Pattern mirror image

Asymmetrical decorative stitch patterns can be reversed to sew from the left or the right.

Pattern extension

This feature expands the stitch pattern to twice its length or more.

Pattern lock

A computerized function, the pattern lock secures the threads at the beginning or end of the stitching line.

Memory

Computerized machines can "remember" designs, alphabets, and phrases. Generally, the memory mechanism is easy to use, and many machines have numerous memories that retain patterns or phases for future use. Refer to your machine's manual for specific information.

The Sewing Machine

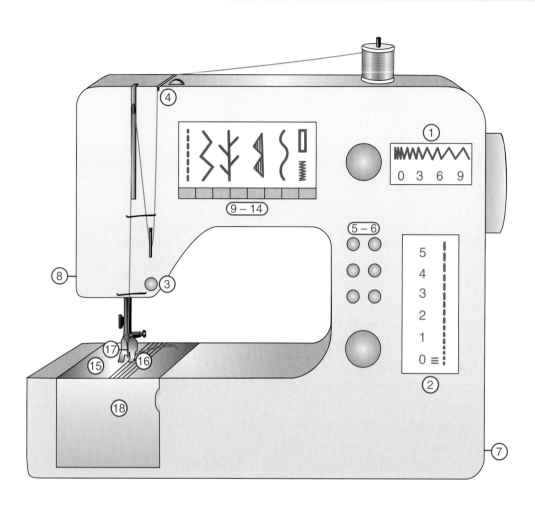

1. Stitch-width adjustment
2. Stitch-length adjustment
3. Reverse stitch
4. Needle-tension adjustment
5. Needle up/down
6. Needle position
7. Feed-dog position
8. Presser-foot pressure dial
9. Motor speed
10. Pattern begin
11. Pattern mirror image
12. Pattern extension
13. Pattern lock
14. Memory
15. Throat plate
16. Presser foot
17. Needle
18. Bobbin compartment

Fig. 2–1.

had a machine with the capacity to "remember" stitches, alter the shape of patterns, and repeat precise needle movements, again and again. The classic mechanical sewing machine, with its primary function of garment and domestic sewing, was forever changed. At first, many stitchers were guarded about the use of such computer gadgets, but within a short time, the consumer was won over by the machine's ease of use, its accuracy, and simple memory recall. The sewer enjoyed the vast capacity of the machine to alter stitch imagery and even, amazingly, to sew alphabets in different sizes—with perfect precision.

Sewing technological advancement exploded in the next 20 years. Increased memory capacity, more stitch-width options, and endless new sewing machine features, such as even-feed, mirror-image, and pattern-begin (press a button and stitch motif restarts at the beginning), made the machine user-friendly. Working side by side with the sewing-machine industry, manufacturers of sewing aids quickly improved their products. High-quality fusible interfacings, stabilizers to support thick thread stitches, and a broad range of thread choices seemed instantly available. What a welcome opportunity for us, as stitchers, to explore creative expression.

Critique Your Machine

You may be in possession of an advanced machine model or a modest version, or you may be in the market for a machine. In the following section, I pose a series of questions and provide some exercises to help you review your machine's potential and explore the market's newest products.

To determine the savvy of your new or old machine, observe it with a detective's eye. Place your sewing machine, sewing manual, all accessory feet, and bobbins on a convenient worktable. Using the following information, analyze your machine and accessories for basic function and flexibility for decorative sewing. Critique your machine both visually and with a simple sewing exercise.

MACHINE FEATURES

First, check your machine to see that it has the features needed for machine crazy patch.

Zigzag dial with a few decorative stitches
Stitch-length dial
Adjustable tension settings
Sewing table
Machine light
Feed-dogs easily changed up or down

MACHINE FEET

There are many types of machine presser feet. The feet shown on page 17 are the ones most often used for crazy patch.

ACCESSORIES

Bobbins. Five or more bobbins are needed for various thread colors and weights.

Machine needles. Buy an assortment of sizes suited to different threads and fabrics.

Brush, oil, tweezers. These items are needed for cleaning and maintaining your machine.

Sewing chair, lamp, table. Select the best you can afford. They will save your back and your eyes.

Sewing Machine Presser Feet

Regular–Necessary
This foot is useful for utility sewing.

Braiding–Optional
The large hole in front of the foot aids in sewing braids and cords.

Patchwork–Optional
This foot is designed to make sewing ¼" seam allowances easy and accurate.

Edge stitch–Optional
A guiding lip aids in sewing perfectly straight seams next to a folded edge, lace, or ribbons.

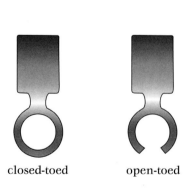

closed-toed   open-toed

open-toed

top side   under side

Darning (free-motion)–Necessary
This foot is designed for use with embroidery and free-motion or outline-style quilting. It is available in several sizes, and can be made of metal or clear plastic.

Embroidery–Necessary
Available in an open-toed or clear plastic style, this foot is the most versatile for crazy embroidery. The foot may be short to increase the visibility of the stitch.

Fig. 2–2.

Crazy-Stitch Exercise

Between the most basic and elaborate machine there are many models. To critique your machine for crazy stitching, sew the following quick exercise. It is designed to help you get acquainted with the full potential of your machine. In addition to teaching you all the buttons, the exercise will stretch your mind toward the creative stitch process.

First, cut a square of plain cotton 12" x 12". Muslin is a good choice. In addition, you will need a sheet of freezer paper or iron-on interfacing, a spool of good quality cotton thread in a color that contrasts with the fabric, and small scissors. If necessary, refer to your owner's manual to complete each task. For the following questions, answer the applicable ones with a yes or no. Sew the appropriate exercises and critique the quality.

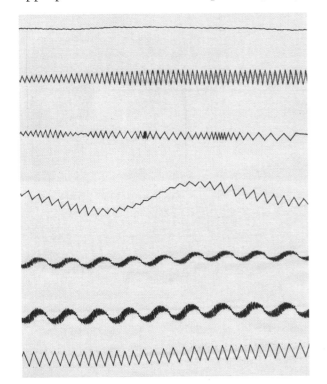

Fig. 2–3. Sewing exercise.

1. **Fill the bobbin and thread the machine.**
   - *Is the machine easy to thread?*
   - *Is the bobbin easy to thread?*
   - *Does the bobbin hold a large amount of thread?*
   - *Did the bobbin fill snugly and evenly?*
   - *Is there adequate sewing machine light?*
   - *Is there a large enough table surface at the same level as the throat plate?*

2. **Put on and take off a presser foot.**
   - *Is this relatively easy to do?*

Set the machine to a straight stitch. Cut the 12" cloth in half, creating two rectangular sections. Fuse the freezer paper or iron-on interfacing to the backs of the sections. For the following exercises, sew rows the width (shortest distance) of the sections (Fig. 2–3).

3. **Sew a row of straight stitches. Change the stitch length from short to long and sew again.**
   - *Is the stitch length easy to adjust?*

4. **Sew a zigzag row next to the straight-stitch row. Change the stitch width and stitch again.**
   - *What is the widest width of the zigzag?*

5. **Try changing the width of the zigzag while you sew.**
   - *Can you change the width gradually while you are sewing?*
   - *Can you also vary the length of the zigzag while you are sewing?*

6. **Explore the other features of the machine.**
   - *Does the needle stop instantly when you take your foot off the foot control?*
   - *Does the needle stop in or out of the cloth?*

- *Can you change this to suit your needs?*
- *Is there a motor speed control, so you can slow the stitch cycle? Sew a row of straight stitches at each speed setting to identify the differences between them.*
- *Can you change the needle position from the center to left and right? How many positions?*

7. Look at the needle-tension dial.
- *Can you change the numbers to achieve a tighter or looser top thread tension? (tighter – higher number, looser – lower number)*

8. Look at the bobbin case.
- *Is there a visible and easily accessible screw available to tighten and loosen the bobbin tension? This is absolutely necessary for sewing thicker decorative threads from the bobbin.*

Machine decorative stitches are usually arranged in units of similar-looking stitches. They are referred to as hand-look, for example feather and briar; cross stitch; compact, which are full-bodied stitches; etc. Whether your machine has a few or many patterns, you can sew an exact image in a repeat cycle, for example, four scallops, or turn a few machine dials and get a variety of results.

9. For this next experiment, select one of the hand-look stitches, which are open and leggy. First sew one row of the selected stitch exactly as it comes from the machine. Look at the stitch sample and consider the quality.
- *Is it attractive?*
- *Is it pucker-free?*
- *Is the bobbin thread hidden underneath the fabric?*

- *Are the stitch width and length attractive for the chosen project?*

If any of the answers are "no," you can find a solution to the problem in one of the following ways:
- *Lightly spray starch and press the fabric to increase body.*
- *Add a strip of tear-away stabilizer underneath the fabric.*
- *Adjust the width and/or length of the stitch pattern.*
- *Resew the decorative stitch with some or all of these aids.*
- *Is there an improvement?*

HINT
- *When the stitch is too wide or too close for the fabric body, the fabric "tunnels." Changing the stitch width and/or length and adding a stabilizer solves the problem.*

10. After reviewing the basic preset decorative stitch, it is fun to explore the machine stitch options to determine the versatility of the various decorative stitches.
- *Change the stitch width and sew again.*
- *Change the stitch length and sew again.*
- *Change the width and length as you sew, curving the stitch row to create a serpentine effect.*
- *Now sew again, in an adjacent row, to explore the stitches' maximum versatility.*
- *If your machine has computerized functions, change the stitch imagery from left to right or vice versa.*
- *Depending on the machine, try other variables, such as sewing the stitch in a single pattern unit or perhaps a half-pattern unit.*

Hopefully, from these simple experiments, you now know more about your machine. These tests were done with a controlled relationship of materials, that is, cotton thread was sewn on cotton fabric. But in crazy-patch embellishment, it is exciting to change threads to get a variety of sheens and thicknesses and to sew on a number of different fabrics. To insure success, refer to the chapter on threads (page 61) and the stitch-tension adjustment test (page 90) to fine-tune the thread-fabric relationship.

Basic Sewing Tools

Fortunately, the basic sewing tools of scissors, rulers, and pencils needed for crazy-patch seem to be in most of our stashes. Although crazy patching doesn't require much more, additional tools are helpful. Listed is a comprehensive grouping with purchasing guidelines. Buy the best you can afford.

Rotary cutter and mat. A rotary cutter contains a round cutting blade, like a pizza cutter but much sharper. This efficient cutter is used with acrylic rulers for cutting strips. Select a rotary cutter in a small, medium, or large diameter. They are available with various types of cutting blades and with different styles of handles.

Scissors. Select a style that feels comfortable and allows you to cut for a long time without fatigue. Be sure the blades meet at the point when you close the scissors.

8"-blade shear. A good shear is designed with bent handles to allow the fabric to lie flat on the worktable during cutting. A selection of quality chrome or stainless scissors will serve you for a long time. If working with a lot of silky-type fabrics, consider buying scissors with one micro-serrated blade and one smooth blade.

4"–5" trimmer. Trimmers, or embroidery clips, are small scissors designed for clipping threads and for close trimming. Styled with a sharp point, the trimmer is ideal for detailed embroidery work.

See-through ruler. A 15" ruler and a square 4" – 6" ruler are necessities. These are only the basics. There are many rulers available. Rulers should be marked in ⅛" increments, and it is helpful if the markings read from left to right as well as right to left. Select rulers with marking colors that show on a wide variety of fabrics and that are particularly suited to your vision. In addition to these basic lengths, consider adding a 60" tape measure, an 18"- or 24"-long ruler, a 12" square, and a triangle.

Fabric marking pens. Markers are available in air-erasable or water-erasable versions. Do not iron over these markings. They may not disappear from the fabric if they are heat-set.

Chalk fabric pencils. Available in white, gray, blue, and yellow, these pencils are wax-free. They are useful for marking the beginning and end of a stitching line. Always draw a line on a scrap of your fabric, then rub the line with the same fabric to be sure the line will disappear. Sharpen these pencils with a hand sharpener.

Powder pounce pouch. The pounce method is useful for marking stenciled quilting patterns. Make a pounce from a 6" square of cotton fabric filled with a small amount of baby powder. Tie the fabric ends to make a little pouch. Place the stencil on your quilt and bounce the pouch on the stencil. The powder will fall through the stencil cut-outs and mark your fabric. Quilt immediately or retrace the powdered line with a chalk pencil because the powder can be rubbed off easily.

Steam iron and pressing cloth. Select the best iron you can afford with a steam hole near the point. The shot-of-steam feature and the extra mister are also helpful. The simplest pressing cloth is often the best. An 18" square of muslin fabric makes a perfect cloth, and a small terry-cloth towel makes an ideal padding for lightly pressing crazy-quilt blocks (face down).

Straight pins. Quilt pins 1¼" long with large heads are recommended.

Straight pin holder. A magnetic holder is handy for crazy patching.

Hand darning needle. The size 18 needle is helpful for threading heavy threads to the back of your work for secure tying.

Thimble. A thimble is largely a matter of choice, but using one enhances stitch quality and saves your finger when used properly; that is, use the side of the thimble to push or receive the needle.

Hand beading needle and thread. Beading embellishment is a grand addition to crazy patch.

Needle Choices

From sewing machine options to needle choices, we can fine tune the relationship of stitch selection to fabric and thread. To accommodate the wide range in thread personalities, the needle industry provides different needle choices. For the best sewing quality, match your needle to the fabric and thread.

For our purposes, only the needles that are most commonly used for machine embroidery are described in the table below. Match the needle to the thread by using the recipe cards on page 64. Always sew with a new, quality needle.

Sewing problems resulting from dull or incorrectly mounted needles include poor thread tension, stressed or striated fabric, uneven pattern units, noisy or clanking stitch cycles, incomplete stitches, and undesirable bobbin thread visibility. When these sewing problems occur, immediately clean the machine, oil the bobbin track, insert a new needle, and check the needle-size-to-thread choice.

Machine Needle Types

Needle	Size	Function
Universal (130/705H)	7/60–19/120	A general-purpose needle, suited to woven and knitted fabrics.
Embroidery (130/705H-E)	75/90	Designed specifically for embroidery thread. Helps eliminate thread shredding and breakage.
Topstitch (130N)	80–110	Larger eye suited to heavier threads.
Metallica (130Met)	80	Specifically designed to stitch metallic threads.
Twin (130/705 H ZWI)	2.0/80–6.0/100	Two needles mounted on one shank to create double patterns of machine embroidery. The first number on the size designation is the distance in millimeters between needles.

Chapter 3
Planning Your Project

varied machine embellishment

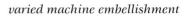

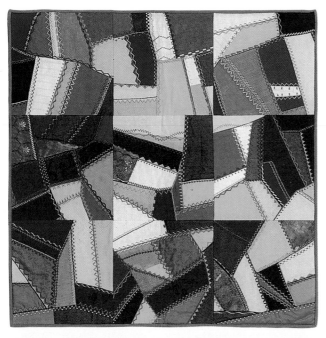

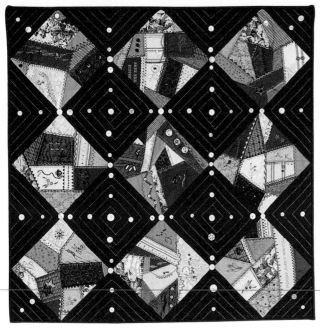

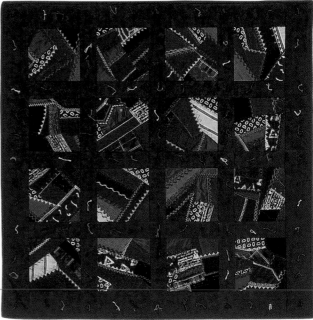

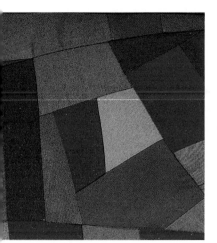

and sew crazy-patch

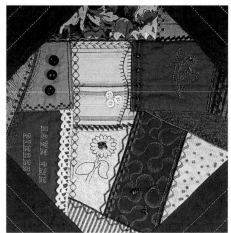

varied machine embellishment

varied machine embellishment

Getting Started

Because we are all different, with varied experiences and skills, we select different starting places. Some of us begin with color or detailed ideas about pattern, size, or embellishment. Others begin with the end project clearly in mind. And sometimes, the project idea merely evolves as we sew, seemingly without any thought. But remember, any and all of these places are realistic beginnings and possess one common denominator—the excitement we feel as we tackle the challenge of a new project. Because of this reality, I've made an effort to organize the material so you can use it wherever you might choose to begin—with supplies or inspiration, with technique or embellishment. Personalize this book for your own beginnings. Flip through the pages and find a starting place that works for you. Go back and forth between the pages. It doesn't really matter. Simply begin at your "getting started" place.

The Idea

Sometimes, a project beginning is fostered by a series of collective experiences, such as the memory of a grandmother's quilt or a special exhibit seen in a museum, gallery, or guild show. At other times, an idea comes from your mind's eye or from a review of your favorite design clippings and sketches. Any of these may serve as a stimulus to a beginning. At first, your memories and notes may seem a menagerie of endless ideas. Are they visual, based on what you've seen? Or do you have an intellectual record, with many notes taken of precise sizes and arrangements? Either and maybe both can serve as a project starter. Sometimes, however, all of your notes and collections of favorite color, stitch, and quilt-style clippings may seem to go in circles and be frustrating, even fruitless. I call this place in the design process "knee deep in mush." Mush is awful. Mushy mud ruins shoes. It annoys. It is unpleasant. A turning point comes as the mush solidifies and becomes more manageable. Thus it is with our quilt projects. If you sort and categorize the pictures and notes, upon close review, you will probably find a kindred connection.

We can't integrate all of our ideas. Some will go by the wayside, some will never solidify, but others will become usable favorites. Separate your favorite ideas. Record their colors, styles, and imagery. Make realistic, decisive fabric and trim choices as you select from your stash. Sketch some simple combinations of ideas, but don't try to finish the design. Leave a door open for surprises, allowing a few questions to lead to a strong and unsuspected ending. Never undervalue the time you spend looking and thinking. It is not time wasted. Ideas from a variety of sources are inspirational, and the visual and intellectual review will stimulate your plans. Each step is encouraging you to go your own direction. Don't worry. Keep thinking and planning. You'll find your way.

Stabilize the "what am I going to do?" by answering some real questions. Plans take action when we answer What size? What colors? What style? What threads and fabrics do I have? Do I need to meet a deadline? Is the project for me? For others? Answer questions candidly and honestly. The answers will simplify your quilt design and, of course, help you make fabric and stitch selections. Forcing yourself into concrete choices strengthens your mind's eye and helps you move forward to a personalized quilt. It solidifies the "mush."

Styles of Crazy Quilt

As you make choices, you are personalizing your crazy-quilt style. Crazy quilts are usually sewn in one of the following ways, whole-cloth or tiled. From these two basic construction methods, it is possible to add sashing, or you can turn blocks on point. In addition, crazy-patch blocks and units can be used in place of other types of patchwork. Explore the quilt style possibilities on the next page.

Styles of Crazy Quilt

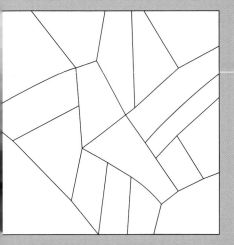

Whole-cloth
The crazy-patch project is sewn on one foundation fabric, such as muslin.

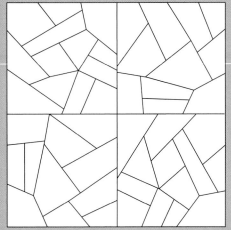

Tiled
Several crazy-patch blocks are sewn together to make a larger quilt.

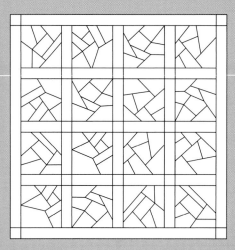

Sashed
Contrasting strips of fabrics are sewn between crazy-patch blocks, adding interest and color.

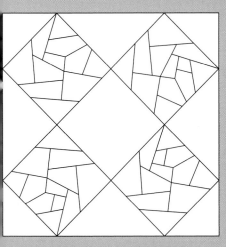

On-point
Several crazy-patch blocks are turned diagonally. Solid or complimentary fabric squares and half-square triangles are added as setting pieces to create a square quilt.

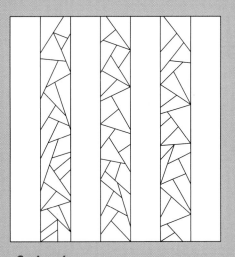

Striped
Crazy-patchwork is sewn to strips of foundation fabric. The crazy-patch strips are sewn alternately with plain fabric strips. The patchwork and fabric "stripes" can be set either straight (above, left) or diagonally (above, right). For diagonal stripes, setting triangles are added to square the quilt.

Styles of Crazy Quilt cont.

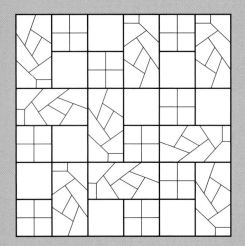

Block units

Crazy patchwork is sewn to foundation pieces to create units to be used in blocks.

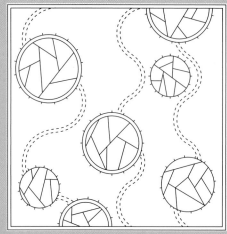

Appliqué

Crazy-patch yardage can be cut into shapes to be used as appliqué.

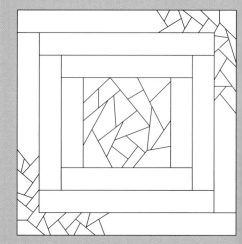

Medallion

Complimentary fabric strips are sewn around a crazy-patch square to create the desired quilt size.

Composition and Size

To decide on a crazy-quilt composition and size, ask yourself these questions: What do I like? What do I not like? How do I see the finished piece? Where do I want to use the crazy quilt? How much time do I have for construction? How much money do I have to buy specific threads and fabrics? Are there special findings I want to put into the quilt, such as buttons, ribbons, and old linens? Is a completion deadline important?

Don't overlook using crazy patches for other things. Try making table toppers, wall-hangings, and bedcovers. Crazy-quilt patches are also attractive in tote bags and small evening bags, funky hats, and garment trims. The variety is endless.

Theme

To develop an original theme in crazy patch is the beginning of personalizing your piece. Themes are simply methods of narrowing the design possibilities. From the "anything goes" theory, it is challenging and fun to place specific limitations on a style. To set a theme, you can restrict your choices to a fabric color or image, such as pastels, plaids, or chickens. Consider incorporating favorite small embroidery units or tatting made by a grandmother. Pull favorite pieces out of the linen chest and incorporate them into a quilt.

The following theme examples may help get you started. But don't stop here. Get out your notes and explore a variety of arrangements with your own ideas.

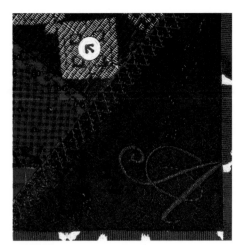

ge multi-motion stitch   *hand-look stitches*   *alphabet*

(See descriptions of types of stitches, beginning on page 76.)

Theme

1 Accented neutrals

Add a color in a tone, tint, or shade to a neutral of black, beige, gray, or white. Find trims and buttons to accent the look.

ACCENTED NEUTRAL, 15" x 15", made by the author.

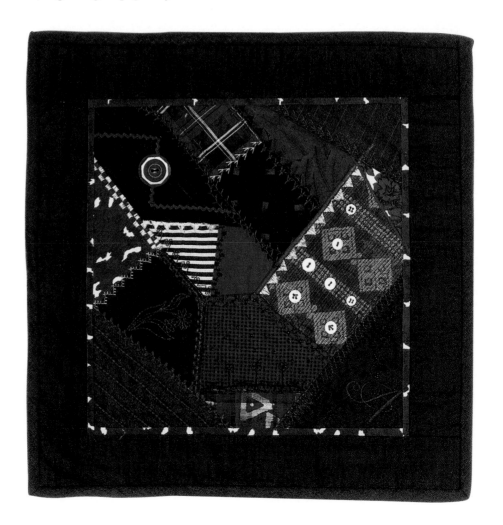

Alice Kolb – **Sew Crazy** with Decorative Threads & Stitches

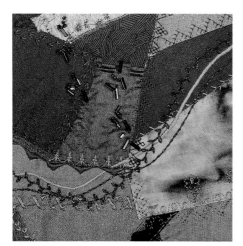

character stitches

compact stitches

hand-look stitches

Theme

2 Japanese silks

Build an arrangement around the elegant presence of a group of treasured fabrics.

JAPANESE SILKS, 14" x 14", made by the author.

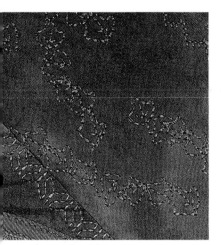

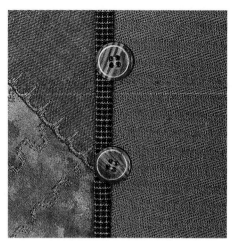

e-motion embroidery   *alphabets*   *edging stitches*

Theme

3 Monochrome treasures

Select one color and work a crazy quilt in the variations of that color.

ANALOGOUS COLORS, 14½" x 14½", made by the author.

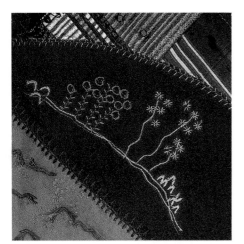

combined stitches to create flowers

compact stitches

alphabet stitches

Theme

④ Traditional crazy

If you have saved family ties for years, consider recycling them into a magnificent quilt.

TRADITIONAL CRAZY, 42" x 42", made by the author.

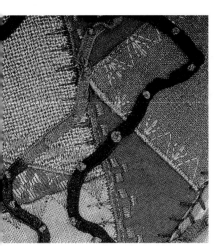

npact stitches   *hand-look stitches*   *compact stitches*

Theme

5 Homestead, etc.

Cutaways of upholstery mixed with other yardages make interesting quilts.

UPHOLSTERY FABRIC WITH TRIMS, 15½" x 15½", made by the author.

compact stitches   *zigzag stitches*   *herringbone stitches*

Theme

⑥ Wildflowers or gardens

Design a color theme from a favorite photo or color print of beautiful flowers. Arrange the fabrics in the same percentages as the colors in the photo.

WILDFLOWERS, 16½" x 16½", made by the author.

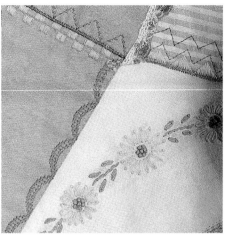

...npact stitches

zigzag and compact stitches

compact stitches, hand embroidery

Theme

7 ## People

Do you have a collection of grandmother's embroidery? Alice selected bits and pieces from her grandmother's stash, then added scraps from her daughter's childhood dresses.

BABY FOUES, 24" x 25", made by the author.

herringbone stitches

compact stitches

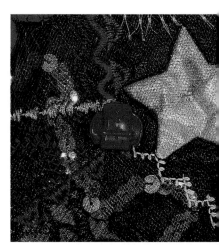

compact and herringbone stitches

Theme

8 Glitzy

Have gorgeous bits of scraps from party dresses? These are perfect for a glitzy quilt. PIZAZZ is a mixture of oddities (fruit net meshing, bottle plastic rings) Fran placed in a serendipitous fashion.

PIZAZZ, 18½" x 18¾", made by guest artist Fran Patterson, Austin, Texas.

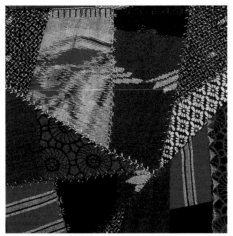

nket stitches   *hand-look stitches*   *hand-look stitches*

Theme

9 Polka dot

Try this jovial and upbeat fabric accented with a heavy embellishing thread. Designed in a simple repetitive image, the variety of silks and simple decorative stitches reinforce the crazy styling.

KANJI CRAZY, 24" x 24", made by guest artist Lorraine Torrence, Seattle, Washington.

compact stitches

compact stitches

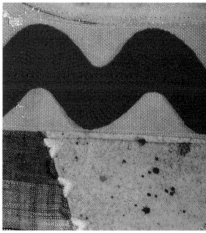

straight stitch

10 Crazy-patch border

Work crazy-patch around a delightful center appliqué. Janet's wall quilt is fourth in her series of similar quilts that try to answer the perennial question, "What's for dinner?"

A CHEESEBURGER 'N PAIRS OF DICE, 22" x 24", made by guest artist Janet Paluch, Sacramento, California.

ltiple stitch options   *edging stitches*   *edging stitches*

Theme

11 Scrap bag mix

For a traditional 1800s style, use scraps from the family collection. From flannel to childhood plaids, bright heavy threads and stylized appliquéd flowers tie the scrap bag mix together.

COUNTRY MEMORIES, 18" x 24", made by the author.

Alice Kolb – **Sew Crazy** with Decorative Threads & Stitches

zigzag stitches

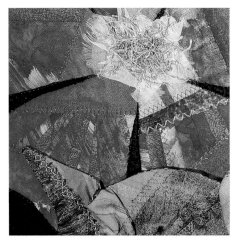

edging stitches

zigzag stitches

Theme

12 Crazy-patch appliqué

Use crazy-patch as appliqué for flowers, animals, geometric shapes, etc. The individual 3-D hot pink floral petals are faced and wired so that each petal can be styled to accent the other.

PRETTY IN PINK, 28½" x 34½", made by guest artist Trish Liden, Camarillo, California.

e-motion embroidery

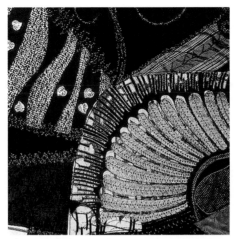

zigzag stitches

free-motion flowers

Theme

13 ## Windows with crazy-patch

Insert crazy-patch in windows of reverse appliqué, then accent with buttons, hearts, embroidery, and curved lines of stitches.

GLEANINGS, 38" x 53", made by guest artist Lucinda Langjahr, Bellevue, Washington.

Theme

14 A favorite print

Buy a variety of fabric prints of chickens, pigs, trucks, Elvis, etc., and style each block from the potpourri of your selection.

CHICK, CHICK, CHICK, 20" x 22", made by the author.

compact stitches 14

14

15

16

17

 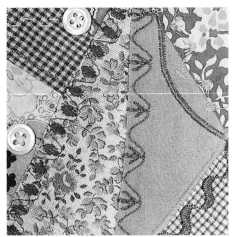 

npact stitches and hand tatting (15)   *hand-look stitches* (16)   *character stitches* (17)

Theme

(15) Buttons & old lace

Mix a collection of old buttons, crochet, or table scarves with favorite neutral fabrics for a nostalgic piece.

BUTTONS & OLD LACE, 20" x 20", made by the author.

Theme

(16) 1930s cotton prints

Perhaps you have some blocks or fabrics from another family member's quilts. Design a crazy quilt around that collection.

'30S REVISITED, 13" x 13", made by the author.

Theme

(17) Redwork

Similar to the traditional hand-embroidery technique, join red and white prints with simple crazy-quilt stitches to your project.

REDWORK SKEW, 22" x 22", made by the author.

quilting stitch

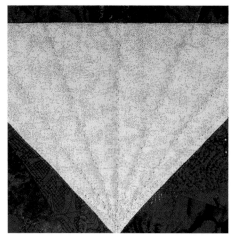

quilting stitch

metallic stitch

Theme

18 ## One decorative stitch

Using high-color contrast, maybe in whole-cloth style, arrange one decorative stitch across a solid piece of fabric, or use the stitch on all the blocks in a quilt. Jane's quilt is a subtle translation of the Lone Star, sewn in multiple crazy pieces of varied red fabrics. Jane enjoys developing the transition in a quiet manner, patching one tiny piece to another.

BIG RED, 28" x 28", made by guest artist Jane Hall, Raleigh, North Carolina.

Theme (continued)

With a theme in mind, a closer look at your fabric selections may strengthen some previous fabric choices and weaken others. A favorite fabric may be tossed aside, while a previously boring selection gains new energy. Look at your colors. Is there a range of attractive colors within your stash? How many shades of red or green or purple do you have? Do you need more? Do you want to include glitzy fabrics, or do you want a tailored, contemporary look sewn in shirtings, flat weaves, and subtle designs? Sort your fabric colors into like groups of reds, purples, etc. Focus on the textures and variety. You can see then if you have enough resources to support your beginning theme.

If a theme still doesn't shout at you, approach your project from another direction. Play mind games to find your idea. Observe and duplicate your surroundings, your weather, or your mood. Refer to colors in a favorite painting. Restrict yourself to a certain size of fabric. Go to the library and look at the artwork in children's books. Buy and duplicate the beauty of fresh flowers. Go to church and sense the beauty of the stained glass windows. Look at the stamps on today's mail. Look at the varied color palette on your dog—his hair, his eyes, and his nose. Wonderful design ideas are everywhere. Set yourself free. Believe in your ideas and do your project your way.

Color

Whatever your theme and your fabric selection, it will be the strength of color that shouts. This energy of color first moved your eyes across a magical kaleidoscope of exhibits and books and stretched your creativity to this point. It is this emotion of color that makes a child say, "My favorite color is pink." And, it is a color force that pushes you into this project and the next. It is intriguing how color intimidates and gives us confidence. Color talks, color communicates.

When I think of color selections, I often think of my favorite childhood book on color, *The Color Kittens*, by Margaret Wise Brown. A beloved book about two playful little kittens discovering color after color, but no green. By happenstance and clumsiness, they discover blue and yellow make green. It was a marvelous discovery that solved all their "color problems." From that moment forward, they had one happy color discovery after another, introducing them to "all the colors of the world." It is this accidental discovery that can work for us. It is an intuitive color sense—the mind's eye knowing that two colors work together.

From this approach, I find it truly does work to select favorite colors with intuition and a sense of "what works with what." But, like many perceptions, a bit of knowledge enhances the thought. Thousands of pages have been written on color and all the theories of color relationships. J.C. LeBlon's wheel of 12 colors is among the most basic of color introductions, and from childhood forward, we have used primary red, yellow, and blue and secondary violet, orange, and green colors, either with an intuitive plan or from LeBlon's academic approach (Fig. 3–1, page 44).

In the paint world, primary colors stand alone. They cannot be mixed by adding other colors, whereas secondary colors are formed by mixing equal amounts of two primary colors. From these primary and secondary colors evolve the tints (lightness of color), the shades (darkness of color), and the tones (grayness of color) that provide endless color

Color Wheel

Fig. 3–1. Color Wheel

Sew Crazy with Decorative Threads & Stitches – *Alice Kolb*

choices. Between primary and secondary colors are the remaining color-wheel choices, the tertiary colors, which also vary in tint, shade, and tone. Today, this simple color primer, a wheel of all the rainbow colors, works as a base for most of us in all of the fabric relationships we create in fashion, craft, and patchwork. Basic knowledge of these specific academic approaches gives us freedom and confidence to approach color instinctively. We do not need an intense study of color. We need only to use color theory as a point of reference. We need confidence to create a framework by using the varied color relationships and to find harmony in our choices.

For a useful color exercise, from the fundamental primary, secondary, and tertiary colors, select a project theme formed on color relationships listed below. This simple approach builds personal confidence in color connections, and it is an adequate insurance policy for success. As you focus on your color plans, look at the color squares in the wheel that were developed by using a wide range of color personalities. Pull your ideas one step closer and build color themes from the basic color palettes.

Monochrome. Many varieties of one color are used in the same piece.

Complementary. These colors lie opposite each other on the color wheel.

Analogous. Choose several colors that are adjacent to one another on the color wheel.

Triad. Select three colors that are equally spaced on the wheel.

Working with these simple categories, you can explore color as personality. Look at reds, purples, and greens. Give each fabric sample a personality adjective, happy, subdued, bold, homey. Keep the personalities of the different color choices friendly, just as we prefer in our own relationships. Let the color personalities interact. For example, place a fabric in a happy tone next to a complementary fabric with a subdued mood.

For another approach, you can build color schemes from the resources around you. Glance through a favorite magazine. Clip pages that have impressive color schemes. Notice the beautiful rooms. Note the ads of beautiful things, not only for their feeling, but also for the strength and compatibility of the connected colors. Maybe a clipping has a bit of brown, red, green, and yellow, with a touch of beige. Look closer at the page. Place fabric colors in order, the most used to the least. This is a quick way to find a color scheme. Could this appealing group of colors be a formula for a crazy quilt? Next, pick up a stack of printed fabrics. Find your favorites and repeat the color exercise, organizing the print from the most used color to the least. Then look at the interaction of the colors. Is the total effect bright, dull, rich, or cool? Find that color harmony in the clipping or fabric. It's an instant color plan.

Are you still uncertain about your color plan? Go to the paint store and collect color chips. Create a swatch book of favorite color combinations from paper, candy wrappers, etc. Match your favorites to actual fabric pieces. Identify color relationships in quilts, clippings, even food presentations. Look at nature and capture the beauty of a garden, a mountain, or a sky. Then tie the color choices to the project intended. Color is an active, vivid part of our stitching world. Explore all its aspects.

Chapter 4

Fabric

A grand mixture, a potpourri, of fabrics randomly sewn in a glistening mix and match arrangement is the image most of us have when we think of crazy-patch quilts. Patches arranged in this manner look like a collage of twinkling lights as fabric textures criss-cross from smooth and dull to plush and shiny. This method of random mixing and matching is the most familiar, but it is only one of several styles of crazy patch, each containing a variety of fabrics with different qualities and care.

Another crazy-patch style is the fabric-theme approach. Selecting specific colors and fabrics within a given theme gives more control, a more predictable outcome of the finished piece. This stitching process is fascinating and results in a beautiful, yet organized crazy-patch style. Regardless of the image you choose, the project attitude (sophisticated, country, whimsical) will evolve from the fabrics selected. Each fabric choice defines your style, even long-term care.

Impulsively, we select the color of patchwork fabric first and consider quality and care second, but, for a moment, reverse this spontaneous manner. Instead, think of the fabric's care and quality—its personality. Every piece of cloth is not only a color, it is also a design (print, plaid, solid), washable or not, and soft or rough in its texture. The fiber (cotton, wool, silk) and weave (broadcloth, satin) define these characteristics. Names of fibers and weaves used interchangeably can be confusing; for instance, using "cotton" to mean broadcloth, but simple consideration of fabric definitions will clear this confusion.

The following chart can help you organize your fabric stash into a useful and meaningful collection. Although there are many fibers and weaves of fabric made into variations from soft batiste cotton to heavy upholstery, I mention only the ones that are proven to work well in crazy-quilt patchwork. Review the chart of the fibers and weaves, then identify the fabrics in your stash. This basic information will be valuable in building quality into your fabric collection for crazy-patching.

Commonly Used Fibers

Fibers (cotton, linen, silk) are the generic names of the fabrics we sew. They help us identify each family group of textiles. The fiber name tells us if the fabric is plant (cotton or linen), animal (silk or wool), or man made (polyester). In addition, fibers generally help us identify a fabric's care and physical qualities (cool, warm, slick).

Cotton

The fabric is made from the ripened fruits (cotton bolls) of the cotton plant. Cotton is a soft, breathable fiber, made into numerous weaves and textures and used extensively for clothing and household fabrics. Sun fades the color.

Common weaves: broadcloth, muslin, percale, twill, velveteen, chintz, sateen, and poplin.

Care: Generally, the fabric can be washed by hand or machine. Hot, warm, or cold water can be used with a mild detergent. Wash dark colors separately in cool water, because bleeding of the dye is common. Slight shrinkage may occur. Soak stained cotton in a vinegar and water solution, then rinse clean. For best results when ironing, use a light mist and a setting of wool to cotton. Spray starch is also helpful.

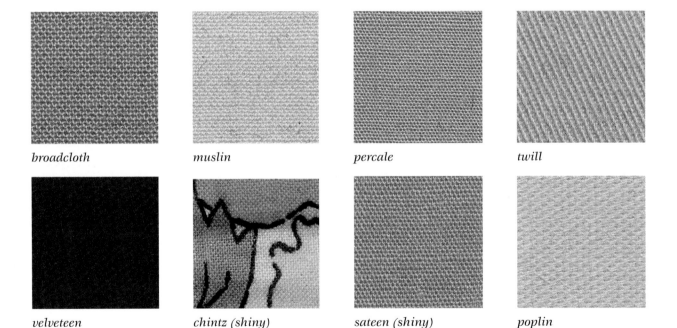

broadcloth   *muslin*   *percale*   *twill*

velveteen   *chintz (shiny)*   *sateen (shiny)*   *poplin*

Linen

The fibers are made from the stalks of flax plants. Linen is stiffer and firmer than cotton. Noted for its texture, it is often used to make clothing and table coverings.

Common weaves: handkerchief, crash, jacquard.

Care: Like cotton, linen is suitable for hand or machine agitation in hot, warm, or cold water with a mild detergent. Stained linen can be soaked in a vinegar and water solution before being washed in a mild detergent. Mist slightly and use the wool to linen setting for ironing. Spray starch is also helpful.

handkerchief

crash

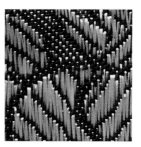

jacquard

Silk

This animal fiber is made from the cocoon of the silkworm. The long filament of the cocoon produces a firm and delicate, yet strong fiber.

Common weaves: duponi, noil, broadcloth, and taffeta.

Care: Silk is washable but fragile. Colors may run, so it's best to wash them separately. The fabric may shrink and it wrinkles. Hand wash silks in mild soap and lukewarm water and hang them to dry. To avoid wrinkles, iron on low heat while still damp. Silk may also be dry cleaned.

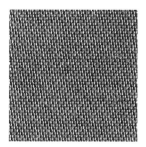

duponi

noil

broadcloth

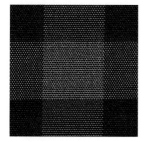

taffeta

Wool

This animal fiber is sheered from sheep. The fibers are relatively short and fuzzy with a natural twist, which hold together in the weave. Wool is warm, yet it breathes.

Common weaves: flannel, twill, tweed.

Care: Dry cleaning is preferable. Occasionally, a gentle soap designed for woolens is appropriate for a sudsy soaking solution. Rinse gently, squeeze out excess water, block and air dry on a towel. Avoid agitation. Press with a dry iron on the wool setting.

flannel

twill

tweed

Metallic

The synthetic fibers are often combined with other fibers in woven or knitted texture. Metallics have brilliant color, found most often in gold, silver, or copper.

Care: Read the label. It is usually dry cleaned.

Novelty fabrics

This category covers a wide range of customized fabrics. The base fabric may be cotton, silk, or rayon. It could be hand woven or machine twisted, and the surface could be embellished with sequins, beads, or appliqués. Novelty fabrics can be commercially manufactured, or they can be designed at home by printing, stamping, bleaching, etc.

Care: Read the label. These fabrics are usually dry cleaned.

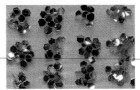

Rayon

This synthetic fiber was developed by scientists seeking a man-made silk. It comes in a variety of weights. It breathes and has a soft "hand."

Common weaves: challis, twill suiting, textured weave, and rayon.

Care: Read the label. Generally, rayon can be hand washed in cool water and machine dried on a low setting. Press with a steam iron set on medium.

challis

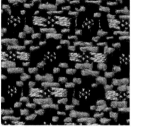
twill suiting

textured

rayon – silk

Acetate

This synthetic fiber is used as an accent. It has a firm drape and makes noise when it rubs against itself. It may split or fade with age.

Common weaves: taffeta, satin.

Care: Read the label. It is usually dry cleaned. If desired, try machine washing and drying the fabric to purposefully alter its appearance.

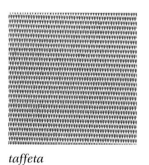
taffeta

satin

Other fabrics

Of course, there are many other fibers, such as polyester and nylon, but they are springy in hand and, most often, not desirable for crazy-patch projects.

Commonly Used Fabrics

Type	Cotton	Linen	Silk	Wool	Acetate	Rayon
Smooth	broadcloth muslin chambray gingham madras	handkerchief	broadcloth taffeta foulard	flannel jersey		challis
Napped	velveteen		velvet velvet brocade			velvet
Ribbed	poplin		poplin faille bengaline			
Shiny	chintz sateen moire		satin moire brocade		satin taffeta moire	
Textured	brocade jacquard damask	crash jacquard	jacquard brocade damask noil	homespun twill tweed		crepe

Metallic fabrics fit into many of the above categories, but they have not been categorized because of the vastness of the selection. Look for brocade, jacquard, damask, and twill.

Testing Fabrics

1. Crush the fabric in your hand. If it has excessive wrinkles that seem to "set," it may be inappropriate for crazy patch or just the look you want.

2. Is the stripe or plaid colored evenly on both sides of the fabric or merely printed on one side? Yarn-dyed fabrics are far superior to printed fabrics for long-term use.

3. Cut a 4" x 4" square and wash it in the manner you expect to wash your finished project. Measure the square. If there has been excessive shrinkage or misshaping, select a different fabric.

Fabrics Weaves

Plain, twill, and satin are the three basic construction weaves of fabric (Figure 4–1). Plain is the most common, while twill is the strongest. Satin is beautiful, but it may be fragile. Two popular variations or fancy weaves include pile (velvet, corduroy) and jacquard (brocade). Identification of the fiber weave and weight (broadcloth, taffeta, damask) is important because these words identify the appearance, appropriateness, and usefulness of a fabric. For instance, silk shantung has texture and it is dressy.

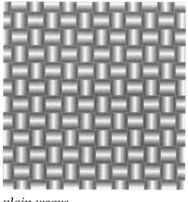
plain weave

twill weave

satin weave

Fig. 4–1. Three basic weaves.

Bengaline

This weave is characterized by pronounced cross-wise ribs formed by bulky, coarse yarns. This heavier version of poplin is beautiful in silk. Grosgrain is bengaline cut to ribbon width.

Broadcloth

This common quilting fabric is a tightly woven, plain weave, lustrous in cotton or silk.

Brocade

The rich, jacquard-woven fabric, in an all-over interwoven design, often contains flowers, pastoral scenes, or foliage. "Brocade" means to ornament. It is a dressy fabric used for home decor, evening wear, church vestments, and formal occasions.

Chambray

The popular cotton shirting and summer clothing fabric is woven with a colored warp (length of grain) and white weft (cross grain).

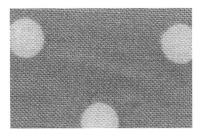

Chintz

This glazed cotton fabric comes in solids and printed figure or floral designs. The glaze may not withstand washing, so be sure to check a small sample.

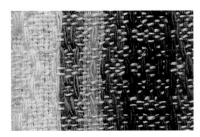

Crash

Made from cotton and/or linen, crash is a neutral, rugged, uneven fabric used for home decorating, decorative jackets, and summer attire.

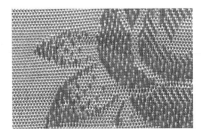

Damask

This reversible fabric is firm and glossy, similar to brocade but flatter. Use it for table linens and summer attire. It can be made from cotton, linen, silk, rayon, or synthetic fibers.

Faille

The weave can have a crosswise rib effect with a soft hand when made in silk or rayon. Faille taffeta has a crisp, stiff cross-rib effect in silk, rayon, acetate, or polyester.

Flannel

Cotton cloth, napped on one or both sides, is used for quilts and clothing. Wool flannels are also common.

Foulard

Popular for dresses, scarves, and men's ties, this lightweight silk or polyester fabric has a soft finish. It is available in plain or twill weave, and contains printed figures across a light or dark background.

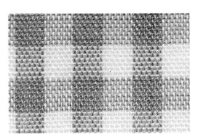

Gingham

Dyed yarns are introduced at even intervals in this plain-weave fabric to achieve block or check effects, ranging from micro to 1" size. Ginghams come in cotton or man-made fibers and are popular in clothing and home decorating.

Handkerchief

The term refers to lightweight, tightly woven cotton or linen. In addition to being used for handkerchiefs, the fabric is also suitable for collars, summer-weight clothing, and decorative home accessories.

Homespun

Available in muted colors of solids, stripes, or plaids, this plain weave is a coarse cotton in a rough-and-ready style.

Jacquard

This intricate style of weaving produces brocade and damask in assorted designs of flowers, pastoral scenes, fictional characters, and real-life imagery.

Jersey

For crazy-patch purposes, jersey is used as a fusible for stabilizing silky fabrics. It is a plain-stitch, knitted cloth.

Madras

The plain-weave cotton is found as stripes, plaids, or small checks of uneven repeat units.

Moire

Recognized as a water-marked finish for formal use, the fabric is available in silk, acetate, or rayon.

Muslin

A cotton cloth of good quality, muslin varies in width from 36" to 102". The word "muslin" implies a neutral or white color.

Noil

The term refers to waste fibers, which are utilized in nubby-textured silk, hence silk noil.

Poplin

The poplin weave produces a fine crosswise-rib effect in cottons. The fabric is used in casual clothing, sportswear, and uniforms.

Sateen

You will find this cotton weave in summer attire and in linings. It has a smooth, lustrous surface.

Satin

This fabric has a smooth, lustrous front and a dull back. It is available in silk or rayon. There are many varieties, including satin crepe, satin lining, slipper satin, double-faced satin, satin damask, and satin taffeta. It is widely used in gowns and dresses, couture, millinery, and home decor.

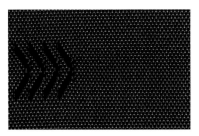

Taffeta

It is a plain, smooth weave with a surface sheen. Its characteristic properties are stiffness and scroop (a grating sound as the fabric moves against itself). It is popular in evening wear, but it may split with age.

Tweed

Noted for its name association with Scottish towns, counties, or battles, this fabric is a rough, irregular, soft and flexible, shaggy woolen, suitable for jackets and outerwear. Examples include Donegal, Harris, and Irish.

Twill

Named for the method of weaving strong, durable goods, this weave is common for sportswear, such as denim, gabardine, and jean cloth.

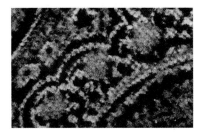

Velvet

This warp-pile cloth has a surface that is very soft, created by successive rows of short cut pile. It is found in hats, garments, wallhangings, and home decor.

Velveteen

This weft-pile cotton cloth has a soft surface with a shorter pile than velvet. Used for children's wear, garments, home decor, and outer garments, it is sturdy and durable.

Crazy-Patch Care

Generally, the finished crazy-patch quilt will not be washable, primarily because of the ornate combinations of piecing, thread, and bead and button embellishment. But the question of the care of individual patch fabrics frequently arises. Precautionary care is an insurance policy against bleeding, shrinkage, etc. Here are some guidelines:

- If you want or need the crazy-patch project to be washable, make fabric choices that are washable and wash everything separately before sewing and embellishing.
- If the project does not need to be washed,

you can sew with random scraps and trims as desired. Occasional dry cleaning may be necessary.

- Consider spraying a new piece with a soil repellent spray.

Buying Fabric

For crazy-patch blocks and units, you can use scraps, but for sashing, borders, etc., the following information will help you determine how much fabric to buy for your project. Keep in mind that most fabrics come in 45" or 52" widths. Usable widths, after the fabrics have been washed and selvages removed, are closer to 40" and 47".

Crazy-patch scraps. Scraps are available from a variety of sources. Buying new fabrics in a fabric store is an obvious choice. Fat quarters, approximately 18" x 20", of broadcloth cotton are readily available in quilt stores. They offer a good way to increase the color and pattern range in your quilts. Other possibilities include yardage from older garments, often found in sale clothing, or yard goods available at recycle stores and garage sales. Look for fabrics at interior design stores and ask about remnants at fabric and drapery stores. If you select recycled fabrics, check for cleanliness and quality. Cut the garments or home decorating units apart and press them, then use as regular yardage.

Consider a minimum variety of five to eight pieces for a small crazy-patch project. If you are creating a large project or want many fabrics, organize your scraps by color. Then texture and quality will be quickly seen, and you can recognize where you need to add selections.

It is easy to start a fabric collection. For many of us, collecting and organizing a stash is the most fun. We enjoy the hunt! Although there are countless fabrics available, selections made from cotton, linen, silk, wool, acetate, metallic, or rayon are the most useful. Educate yourself about the names and textures of fabrics (see pages 48–56), and remember to always check the fabric for quality. Never use fabric that is weak, badly torn, or stained. Avoid the near rotten, no matter how beautiful it is. The perfect treasure is waiting. Simply buy small amounts of old and new fabrics in various markets and never feel guilty.

Sashing. Fabric strips cut and sewn between each crazy-patch block and row are called "sashing" strips. Use the following method to determine sashing yardage, based on cutting strips selvage to selvage:

1. Using cut sizes (includes seam allowances), add up the lengths of all the vertical and horizontal sashes. If the horizontal sashes need to be pieced, be sure to add fabric for the extra seam allowances.

2. To find the number of strips that need to be cut across the fabric (selvage to selvage), divide the combined length of all the sashes by the usable fabric width.

3. Multiply the number of fabric strips needed by the desired sash width; include ½" for seam allowances. This number is the total length, in inches, of fabric required.

4. Divide the total inches by 36" to find the number of yards.

5. You will probably want to buy ⅛ or ¼ yard extra for insurance.

Borders. You can use one border or several to frame your crazy patch. For this yardage estimate, it is assumed that the border strips are 10" wide or less, and the border lengths are cut parallel to the selvages. The corners can be mitered or butted.

1. Measure the longest side of the project, including seam allowances.
2. Add 6" for insurance, which gives you the total number of inches.
3. Divide the result by 36" to find the number of yards.

Backing. If your crazy-patch project is narrower than 36", you can use one panel of 40"-wide fabric for your foundation. If the project is wider than 36", you will need three panels. Cut the yardage in half, selvage to selvage, to make the two panels. Cut one of the panels in half lengthwise. Sew the half panels (minus selvages) on either side of the whole panel. Trim the excess backing after pinning the layers.

Use the following formula for determining backing yardage. This formula can also be used for buying foundation fabric for a whole-cloth crazy patch.

1. For projects narrower than 36", buy yardage to equal the length of the piece plus 4" for ease in layering the quilt top, batting, and backing.
2. For projects wider than 36" but narrower than 70", buy fabric twice the length of the project plus 4".
3. For projects wider than 70", buy fabric three times the length of the project plus 6".
4. Divide by 36" to find the number of yards.

Binding. The strips for binding the raw edges of your quilt can be cut on the straight of grain or the bias. I prefer to cut them on the crosswise straight of grain. The strips will have a slight amount of stretch but not as much as a bias cut. A double-fold binding is very serviceable for a quilt, providing protection and life to the project. Cut the binding four times the desired finished width, plus ½" for a seam allowance. For instance, for a ½" finished width double-fold binding, figure the cut width at 2½" (4 x ½" = 2" + ½" = 2½").

1. Measure the length and width of your quilt and add the two measurements together.
2. Multiply the result by 2 to find the total measurement around all four sides.
3. Add 12" for turning corners and finishing the ends.
4. Divide the total by 40" to find the number of strips to cut across the fabric, selvage to selvage.
5. Multiply the number of strips by the cut width of the binding, 2½" in the example.
6. Divide the result by 36" to find the number of yards.

Backing Yardage
(fabric at least 40" wide)

Quilt	Size	Backing Yards
Crib	42" x 58"	3⅝
Twin	67" x 89"	5½
Double	81" x 89"	8⅓
Queen	88" x 94"	8¾
King	100" x 98"	9⅛

Planning Chart

Make a copy of the following chart for each of your projects to help you plan and track your quilts.

Planning Chart

Project _____

Theme _____

Size _____

Yardage _____

Scrap colors _____

_____

_____

_____

Sashing _____

Backing _____

Binding _____

Colors _____

_____

Threads _____

_____

Machine accessories and feet

_____

_____

Sewing tools _____

_____

_____

Fabric Choices

Chapter 5

Threads and Stabilizers

Threads

Like our fabric choices, thread selection is first made by color. However, the color choice is but one factor in the success quotient of the thread design on the patchwork. Thickness, sheen, needle choice, even the stitch selection, make a world of difference in the "attitude" of the chosen thread. I often speak of thread attitude, because, by its very nature, the word fits. We've all sewn a decorative stitch that looked great, and we've all had disastrous results. Most of our success or failure with thread is directly related to the mixture we put together: the selection of thread color to fabric, thread selection to needle size, the type (if any) of fabric stabilizer, and the stitch selection.

Look at the scope of your thread selection possibilities. There are countless colors of every fiber and an endless variety of thicknesses and sheen in cotton, rayon, metallic, and synthetic threads. The greater the variety, the more interesting the crazy-stitch embellishment. It makes sense to simplify these choices. First, become familiar with your inventory of thread.

Select threads that match your fabrics in addition to threads that obviously mismatch, for instance, bright orange and pastel pink. Organize a wide range of color choices. Place the threads flat on a small jelly-roll pan or serving tray so the colors can be easily seen. Do not try to select color from a box of neatly arranged threads set on end. What threads do you have that are bright and shiny? Dull and opaque? Thick and thin? What other thread textures do you have that lend themselves to couching, dimensional embellishment, or accents? You can rarely have too many threads, so be generous in your selections.

Separate your inventory into fiber types: cotton, rayon, etc., by reading each spool label (Fig. 5–1). Within the fiber groups, identify and separate your threads by their physical appearance: shiny or dull, thin or thick, and metallic. Use the thread table (Thread Fiber Types) to identify and group your threads in categories of fiber, style, and brand; for example, cotton, silk-finish, Mettler. We need this information to match our thread choices to the fabric, the needle thread, bobbin thread, and needle. If this matching is ignored, we often have a frustrating embroidery experience. Later, we will use a second table to create a recipe for the sewing machine, to coordinate the needle thread with the bobbin thread and the needle. Acquire threads from all the groups, in the color range you use most often. The greater the variety, the more interesting the crazy-stitch embellishment.

Bobbin Threads

If you are using decorative thread in the needle, you will need to choose a more utilitarian bobbin thread. Generally of neutral color, it should not show in the decorative stitch on the fabric surface. The following examples are thin, but strong, threads specifically designed for this use. See page 64 for information on matching the needle, needle thread, and bobbin thread.

Bobbin Threads

FOR FINE NEEDLE THREADS

Brand	Style
YLI	Lingerie/Bobbin
Madeira	Bobbin-fil

FOR THICK NEEDLE THREADS

Brand	Style
Mettler	Metrolene 120-wgt. polyester
Mettler	Polyester – ideal bobbin thread for top-stitched decorative threads

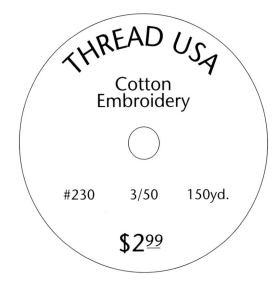

Fig. 5–1. Be sure to read spool labels.

a variety of bobbin threads

Thread Fiber Types
(a partial list)

Brand	Style	Brand	Style
COTTON		**POLYESTER**	
Mettler	Silk Finish	Mettler	All-Purpose
	Embroidery 30/40 wgt.		Cordonnet
	Pearl		
		YLI	Jean's Stitch
Madeira	Tanne 30/40 wgt.		
	Cotona	Guttermann	Top stitching
		METALLIC	
YLI	Quilting Thread	Sulky	Lightweight
			Sliver
DMC	Lightweight Cotton 50 wgt.		
RAYON		Madeira	FS Jewel
Sulky	30/40 wgt.		Supertwist
	Ombré		
		Kreinik	Blending Filament
Madeira	40 wgt.		
	Graduated Hues	Coats	Lightweight Twist
Coats	40 wgt.	**WOOL/ACRYLIC**	
		YLI	Monet
YLI	Pearl Crown		
	Ribbon Floss	Madeira	Burma Lama
Coats	Color Twist (two colors)	Sew/art	Renaissance
Isacord	Embroidery 40 wgt.	**TINSEL**	
		Sulky	Sliver
Robison-Anton	Embroidery 40 wgt.		
BLENDED OR WRAPPED		Coats	Glitz
(polyester and cotton)			
Coats Dual Duty	All-purpose	Madeira	Jewel
	Top stitching		
	Extra Fine	Glisser	Gloss Prizm Hologram
YLI	Jeans Stitch	Madeira	Neon
Guttermann	Top stitching		
Madeira	Top stitching		

Which Thread and Needle?

Thread, needle, and decorative stitch selection—it truly seems like the old story, "Which comes first, the chicken or the egg?" Perhaps there is no specific order for making these selections, but if one segment is out of sync, often the total thread-decorative stitch process becomes annoying. To give order to this sequence of events, you can organize decorative threads into three groups: lightweight, medium-weight and bobbin-weight. For each of these categories, a recipe card is provided to help you coordinate the needle, thread, and bobbin thread. These recipes can reduce the frustrations of thread breakage, poor stitch quality, and so on, caused by the mix and match of incorrect products. Try these recipes. I think they will work for you.

lightweight decorative threads

medium-weight decorative threads

bobbin-weight decorative threads

Recipe Cards

Light-weight Decorative Threads

These threads are often used for satin-stitch appliqué and for quieter, softer thread imagery. They are also ideal for dense, compact decorative stitches.

Needle	**Needle Thread**	**Bobbin Thread**
Universal (130/705H) size 70/80	COTTON:	Same as in needle or a utility thread:
Embroidery (130/705 H-E) 75/90	Mettler silk finish, embroidery	YLI lingerie and bobbin, also fine, clear nylon
	Coats, extra fine	Mettler 60 wgt. cotton
	DMC, 50 wgt.	Metrolene (polyester)
	RAYON:	Madeira Bobbin-fil
	Sulky	Sew-Art Sew-Bob
	Madeira	Clear nylon
	Coats	

Medium-Weight Decorative Threads

These threads show more boldly on fabric. Select a larger-eyed needle to match the thicker thread and stronger bobbin thread.

Needle	Needle Thread	Bobbin Thread
Top-stitch (130N) size TOP-100	METALLIC	Polyester all-purpose
Metallica (Met) size 75/90	Madeira	Cotton-covered polyester all-purpose
	Mettler	
	Sulky	
	Coats	
	YLI	
	PLIED COTTON/POLYESTER	
	(Top stitching)	
	Mettler, Cordonnet/polyester fiber	
	YLI, Jeans	
	Guttermann, top stitching	
	Coats, top stitching	

Bobbin-Weight Decorative Threads

When a thread has too soft a twist or is too thick for the needle's eye (often looks like a paint-brush at the cut end), it is best sewn from the bobbin. A strong inconspicuous support thread is then sewn from the needle, or if desired, a decorative medium-weight thread is sewn from the needle to engage a double impact of thread color.

Needle	Needle Thread	Bobbin Thread
Universal (130/705H) size 70/80	Mettler, polyester all-purpose	Madeira Décor, rayon
Topstitch Needle (130N) size TOP-100 (for the topstitch threads)	Coats, cotton covered polyester	Madeira Glamour, metallic
	Topstitch, refer to the medium-weight card	Madeira Carat, rayon and metallic
		YLI Candlelight, metallic
		YLI Pearl, rayon
		Ribbon Floss, rayon and metallic
		DMC Pearl, cotton
		Kreinik Braids, metallic

Stabilizers

A stabilizer is a secondary product (additional fabric, iron-on film or fabric, or starch) that firms the hand (increases the body) of the crazy-patch fabric to make it more receptive to quality machine stitching. Stabilizers help balance the stretchiness and thickness of adjoining fabrics. It can be as unnoticeable as spray starch misted across the fabric surface to temporarily improve fabric body or as permanent as a fusible fabric applied to the underside of a patch before it is sewn to a muslin foundation. In addition, tear-away stabilizers are used extensively under decorative stitches to improve the fabric hand and give more control to the decorative stitch imagery. This product is literally torn away or cut away after the stitch work has been completed.

Commonly Used Stabilizers

Spray starch. A light mist of spray starch across the surface of a patch will give it temporary body and hand, which is ideal for short-term use. Assorted brands are available in the detergent section of most grocery stores and super markets.

Knit fusible. This thin, knit yardage has a light film of fusible glue on the surface. It must be preshrunk for best results. Wispy, lightweight fabrics, such as sheer silk or men's tie fabric, are much more easily controlled when a fusible knit interfacing is applied to the back before sewing the patches to a muslin foundation. This fusible stays on the silk permanently, adding a subtle layer to the patch and making it much more manageable.

Cut random pieces of the silky fabrics, then fuse them to a ½ yard of preshrunk knit interfacing. Cut random patches from the knit unit as needed. To preshrink a knit fusible, immerse it in a basin of warm water for 30 minutes. Squeeze the excess moisture from the fabric and hang it over a towel rack to dry. *Assorted brands:* HTC Fusi-Knit, HTC So Sheer, Stacy Easy Knit, and French Fuse.

Woven fusible. This is a lightweight fabric, much like batiste, that has a light film of fusible glue on the surface. This fusible is ideal for use under heavily embroidered pieces. The extra hand of the lightweight fusible enhances monograms and single-motif embroidery. It keeps the dense thread work smooth and helps to prevent stitch tunneling and waving.

To use a woven fusible, fuse an assortment of cut fabrics, suited for centered machine embroidery, to the lightweight fusible. Cut apart units as needed. *Assorted brands:* HTC Form-flex All Purpose and Stacy Shape-Flex.

Tear-away products. These felted products are designed to be pulled or cut off the background fabric after stitching has been completed. There are many on the market, so try several brands to find your favorite.

To use a tear-away, cut a strip or square of the product and place it just under the area to be stitched. After stitching, cut the product away close to the stitched edge. Be aware that pulling may distort the stitches. Use 1" strips of the product centered under seam edges that will be embroidered. *Assorted brands:* Stitch and Ditch Stabilizer, Swedish Tear Away Paper, Sulky Stiffy, Jiffy Tear Away, and Sprayway Fabric Stiffener.

Stabilizer Summary

Muslin. This plain cotton fabric is used as a foundation for applying crazy patches.

Woven fusible iron-on interfacing. Use as a medium support under fabric. Ideal for appliqué and monogramming and dense embroidery.

Knit fusible interfacing. Use under tie fabric, lightweight silk, or rayon fabric to provide light body and keep the fabrics from floating (rising between the seams).

Tear away. Cut the stabilizer in strips to be used under decorative stitch rows to balance the stress of dense stitching.

Chapter 6

Straight-Stitch Appliqué

As with all sewing projects, many methods are used to sew crazy patch. Sewing one patch at a time to a foundation or sewing in the popular flip-and-sew method are but two of the many ways to sew bits and pieces of fabric into a colorful arrangement. I prefer a third technique, that of straight-stitch appliqué. Each patch is simply pinned to a muslin background, then machine straight stitched along the patches' edges, securing them to the background. It is also possible to combine the one-patch, flip-and-sew, and straight-stitch appliqué methods in one project.

Straight-stitch appliqué is ideal for machine crazy patch because it secures the decorative fabric to the muslin and creates a smooth surface and guide line for the decorative seam embroidery. Better yet, the decorative machine embellishment hides the line of straight stitches. Lastly, accents of lace, old buttons, ribbons or nostalgic personal mementoes, such as charms, and beads add flare to each piece.

Supplies for Straight Stitch Appliqué

Yardage
Background muslin cut to desired size
Assorted fabrics for patchwork
Assorted fabrics for sashing and borders (optional)

Threads
COLOR: neutral blending thread in two colors
   light beige or gray to match light-valued fabrics
   dark to match dark-valued fabrics
NEEDLE THREAD: fine nylon, polyester, or
   all-purpose cotton
BOBBIN THREAD: thin and strong or match to
   needle thread

Sewing tools
Sewing machine with straight stitch
Sewing foot – open-toed or clear embroidery
Steam iron and pressing pad
Scissors – 8" shears and 4"–5" trimmers
Straight pins (quilter's long pins are ideal)
Rotary ruler
Rotary cutter and mat (optional, but useful)
Hand needle and thread (useful for hand basting
   hard-to-manage fabrics)

General Procedure

Organize a table wide enough for three areas of work: **1.** fabric sorting, cutting, and patching; **2.** iron and pressing pad; **3.** sewing machine. When the work area is conveniently arranged in a sequential order, the process goes much faster.

Working from ideas developed in Chapter 3 (page 22), select a collection of fabrics for your chosen theme and style. Arrange your colored fabrics on the table in like color groupings at the back of the sorting and patching area. From your sorting area select a fabric. Use the following instructions to cut, press, and pin the patches to muslin. Refer to Chapter 9 (page 110) for suggested projects, sizes, and yardages.

Adding Patches to Muslin

1. Cut a pressed muslin foundation at least 2" larger than the desired finished size. Place the foundation on the work table.

2. Select fabric #1. Cut a scrap in an odd shape. One way to create an odd shape is to cut a square, then trim one corner diagonally. Pin the shape to the center or to the corner of a muslin foundation (Fig. 6–1).

3. Select fabric #2. Fold and press under a ¼" allowance along one edge. Place the turned under edge over the first patch as desired (Fig. 6–2). Trim away any extra fabric under the second patch, leaving about a ¼" overlap.

4. Select fabric #3. Fold and press under a ¼" allowance along one edge. Place #3 over one or both of the previous patches. Pin in place.

5. Repeat until the muslin is covered (Fig. 6–3a). If you have some problems, refer to the Tips for Troubles section on page 70.

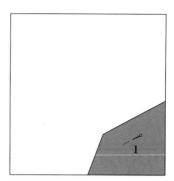

Fig. 6–1. Patch #1 pinned in the corner.

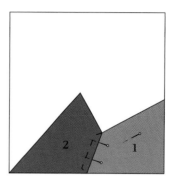

Fig. 6–2. Fold under the seam edge of patch #2 before adding it to patch #1.

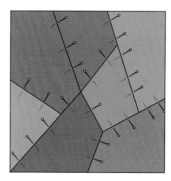

Fig. 6–3a. Cover the muslin with patches.

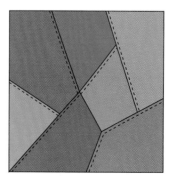

Fig. 6–3b. Stitch the patches to the muslin.

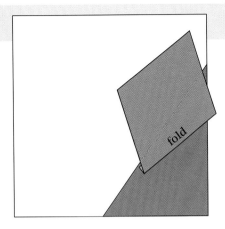

Fig. 6–4. To reshape a patch, place one on top at a steeper angle.

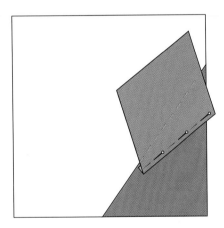

Fig. 6–5. Align pins with the fold.

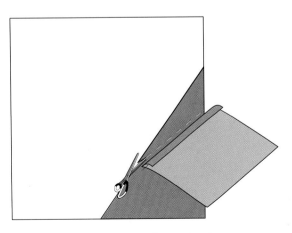

Fig. 6–6. Lift the top patch to trim the bottom one.

6. When the muslin is covered with pinned decorative patches, you are ready to straight-stitch appliqué (Fig. 6–3b, page 69).

Tips for Troubles

Reshaping a patch. Using a steeper angle, position a patch on top of the one to be reshaped (Fig. 6–4). Pin the top patch in position with the straight pins aligned with the fabric fold (Fig. 6–5). Then lift the top patch and trim the excess fabric from the bottom patch (Fig. 6–6).

Bulky fabric. If the selected fabric is too thick to turn a ¼" seam allowance, simply place the thicker piece flat on the muslin. Then place lighter-weight fabrics with folded seam allowances over the bulky patch. Avoid trying to do a total project in thick fabric. Instead, mix the brocades and tapestry weights with the lighter weights.

Curves. Occasionally, you may want a curved patchwork shape. An easy way to control a curved shape and avoid a pointy curve is with a technique I refer to as a stitched weight line. Cut the desired curved-shape patch, including a ¼" seam allowance. With your sewing machine set at a length of 2½ mm, sew a straight-stitch line ¼" away from the curved edge. The single stitch line provides a guide for folding the curved shape

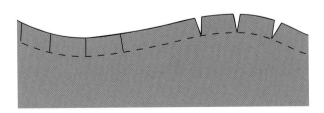

Fig. 6–7. Clip curves, if needed.

gracefully, without points. Finger press the curved shape along the stitching and pin it to the muslin. If the curve needs help, clip up to but not through the stitching line, clipping about every ½" (Fig. 6–7).

Adding trim. To add a lace trim, rick-rack, braid, etc., to the edge of a patch, insert it at the time of pinning. Insert the cut seams of the trim under the folded patch edges. Then sew the patch and insertion trim to the muslin at the same time.

Slippery and floating fabrics. Lightweight tie fabrics, silks, and rayon often slip and slide or float (won't lie flat) when placed next to thicker fabrics on a muslin foundation. Prevent this problem by first fusing a lightweight knit interfacing to the back of the silky fabrics. Then cut and place the interfaced fabric on the muslin.

HINT

* *Stabilize several silky fabrics at once by placing multiple scraps on a larger piece of knit fusible interfacing. Fuse all the silky pieces to the interfacing, then cut and patch each piece, as needed, from the stabilized fabrics.*

See-through fabrics. If a fabric is sheer and the underneath fabrics show through, try interfacing it. Fuse a piece of knit or woven interfacing to the backside of the sheer, then apply the fabric to the muslin.

Embroidered patches. Patches with large or singular embroidered designs are easier to insert into a crazy-patch project when the embroidery is first stitched on an individual fabric unit, then trimmed as needed, to fit the patch area.

HINT

* *Be sure to cut stabilized fabric patches larger than needed. Embroider a design in the center, then trim the patch to fit. Always machine embroider on a stabilized fabric. A tear-away stabilizer may also be needed to keep the thread work from tunneling.*

Sewing the Appliqué

Thread the sewing machine with a blending thread, one that shows the least across all the fabrics. A lightweight nylon, cotton, or polyester in taupe, beige, or gray is usually a good choice for the needle with a lightweight gray or beige in the bobbin. Set the machine at the straight stitch with a length of 2½–3 mm. Place the sewing needle at a patch fold at the outer edge of the muslin. Sew about ¹⁄₁₆" in from the folded edges of the patches, in a continuous line from one patch to the other (Fig. 6–8). Sew as far as possible following the patch edges, without stopping. As necessary, start and stop with a neat, securing stitch. You can backstitch about two to three stitches or use an auto-lock feature to secure the threads. After continuous-line sewing the long patch seams, use straight-stitch along the short seams that cannot be connected in a continuous line (Figs. 6–9a and b, page 72).

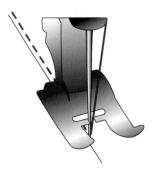

Fig. 6–8. Sew about ¹⁄₁₆" from the folded edge.

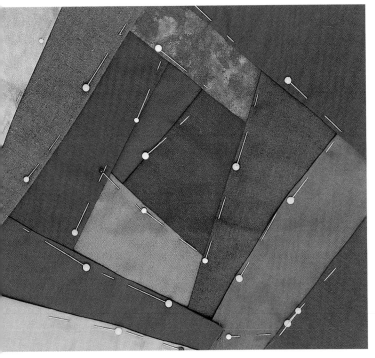

Fig. 6–9a. Pin the patches to the foundation.

Fig. 6–9b. Straight-stitch patches to the foundation.

Fig. 6–10. Machine embroidery will hide the straight stitches.

HINT

• *Occasionally, it may be necessary to change thread colors from light to dark. Always use the thread that shows the least. If the thread color shows more than desired, don't fret. The straight stitch will become inconspicuous when the decorative stitches are applied (Fig. 6–10).*

Hints for Each Quilt Style

SEE PAGE 25 FOR CRAZY QUILT STYLES

Whole-cloth. Crazy patch is sewn to one piece of support fabric that is the size of the project plus 6" more in width and length. It is recommended that whole-cloth projects not exceed 50"–55". Larger units than this are difficult to manage in the decorative machine embroidery process. If you need a larger finished piece, work in tiles, stripes, or on point.

Patchwork tiles. For each square, cut one preshrunk muslin piece, on the straight of grain, that is the finished size plus 2" more in width and length. Cut as many squares as needed to construct the project. Sew patches to each square. After the embroidery work has been completed, cut the individual squares to the desired size, including seam allowances, before sewing them together.

Combined patchwork styles. You can combine crazy patch with appliqué, plain squares, or simple patchwork. For instance, a crazy patch unit can be used as one component of a block. Sew each style of unit, appliqué, four-patch, etc., individually, then join the units to complete a block.

Sashing. Contrasting strips can be placed between crazy-patch blocks to create a frame around each one. Crazy patch each square, following general procedures. After embellishment is completed, cut each muslin square the desired size plus seam allowances. Cut sashing strips the desired width and use the block measurement to cut the sashing strips to length. Remember to include seam allowances in the width and length of the strips. Sew the crazy-patch blocks together in rows, inserting sashing between the blocks. Insert a long sashing strip between each crazy-patch row.

Stripes and crazy patch. Solid-colored lengthwise fabric strips can be placed between rows of crazy patch. Cut and sew crazy-patch strips the desired size plus seam allowances. Sew the strips together, inserting vertical or diagonal contrasting strips between the crazy-patch strips. If sewing on the diagonal, cut half-squares for the two short corners.

On-point. Crazy-patch squares can be turned on point, with solid-colored squares sewn in between and in the corners. Cut crazy-patch and solid fabric squares the same size, including seam allowances. Sew them together in rows, alternating the solid and crazy-patch squares. Sew half-squares to the border edges.

Medallion. Cut border strips the desired size plus seam allowances and sew them to a crazy-patch square, through the muslin foundation. You can sew the borders Courthouse Steps-style, that is, sew border strips to both sides first, then to the top and bottom for each round of borders. Add enough borders to the medallion to fill the muslin square.

Jackets and vests. An outerwear jacket or vest of crazy patches can be sewn to a muslin foundation to ease construction and embellishment. Cut preshrunk muslin in a rectangular shape for each front, the back, and the sleeves. Trace each jacket pattern shape on the muslin with a water-soluble marking pen. Add crazy patches to the muslin. Be sure to match the appliqué lines of the patches as they fall across the center front. Extend the piecing about 3" past the traced line on each muslin piece. Trim each section to the desired garment shape after embellishing.

Chapter 7

Embellishments

Machine Embroidery

The stitch, as we know it, evolved slowly, from connecting crudely styled animal skins to the modern needle and thread techniques we recognize today. Increasing skill and knowledge, along with the desire to invent or share stitches, expanded the basic stitch into decorative variations. Improved materials and supplies complemented these advancements, and the decorative flourishes added to function became known as embroidery.

Just as the twist of the hand needle gave us the first recorded embroidery stitch, the swing of the machine needle from left to right gave us the first zigzag or decorative machine stitch. A series of changes pushed the decorative stitch into myriad images, from a simple zigzag to complex honeycombs, even to cross-stitched thread arrangements. Many new sewing machine models sport an enormous number of these designs. In addition to these automated stitches, today's sewer has the basic flexibility of changing tension, width, and length. She can sew with fine or thick thread, and if using a computerized machine, she can select a variety of machine options, such as mirror image and pattern begin.

Supplies

- Quality sewing machine
- Sewing feet
    standard
    embroidery
    darner for free-motion
    edge-stitch
    braiding
- Machine brush and oil

- Assorted needles
- Seam ripper
- Small screw driver
- Spare light bulbs
- Scissors, 8" and 4"–5"
- Straight pins
- Large-eyed hand needle
- Machine embroidery hoop

PLANNING STITCHES

Planning sewing machine stitches on your crazy quilt is easier if time is first spent reviewing some books on hand stitches used on old crazy quilts (see Resources, page 142). Then compare your machine's index of stitch styles to your favorite hand stitches. You'll see a reflection of the past as it corresponds to the modern technology, and most importantly, endless opportunities for personalizing crazy patch. To enhance your awareness of stitch variations, it is helpful to sew samples of the stitches, always first in basic form, then altered with as many options as imaginable.

Look at machine stitches with an analytical eye. View the shape, the size, and the stitch density. Stitches with straight or angular lines feel more tailored and straightforward, while curved, looped, or skewed stitches soften or connect a surface area. Stitches with themes of hearts, bows, and scallops add a feminine touch, while jagged triangles, diamonds, and arrows add masculinity and color density to a sampler. Think of stitches as personalities and select accordingly.

Within the stitch considerations is another serious option, the wide variety of styles and moods achieved by thread selection. Color is an obvious decision, but texture and sheen are perhaps equally important. High-sheen colored thread produces a contrast to the fabric texture, while the dull, opaque colors hold closer to the background. Thin threads, both shiny and dull, show less in coarsely woven or thicker piled fabric, while thicker threads, both shiny and dull, ride on the fabric surface and show themselves strongly across the patches. Integrated, the patch, stitch, and thread color and the thickness and sheen dictate the mood of a project and reinforce or scramble the desired theme.

TYPES OF STITCHES

Although various machine brands label stitches differently, they all fall into kindred categories. Some machines will have all of the categories. Others will have only a few. Usually, the decorative stitch choices are arranged in a display panel on the machine and in the machine manual. Listed are the primary stitch styles identified by generic headings. Read the text and study the line drawings to expand your perception of each stitch's potential.

Straight stitch

This is the most familiar stitch on the machine. It is rarely thought of as a decorative stitch because it has always filled the task of dependability in sewn clothes and domestics. But decorative power it does have, following the style that you give it. The imagery can be varied depending on the spacing of the stitches, choice of thread, and the relationship of the rows to each other. Silk or rayon thread sewn on a smooth and tightly woven surface, such as handkerchief linen, reflects a delicate, sophisticated repetition, while a coarse top-stitching thread sewn on a textured hopsacking is informal and casual in mood and interpretation. The straight stitch strengthens when sewn in rows, it accents when sewn as an echo around an appliqué, and if scrolled across another seam, it adds rhythm to the patch. In hand embroidery, the closest stitch to the machine straight stitch is the running stitch. Use the straight stitch often, in varied threads and relationships.

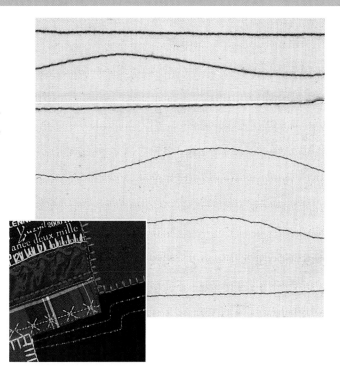

Zigzag

Recognized as a stitch that angles back and forth in a slightly slanted position, the stitch is made by the needle moving the same distance from the center position to the left, then to the right. With adjustment knobs, the stitch width and the length can be changed. In its wide range of choices, the zigzag is among the most basic of decorative stitches, but it offers endless variety, depending on thread choices and stitch setting. Try the zigzag down a row in an expected width and length. Try it again, turning the width knob from wide to narrow, then back again, as you sew. The zigzag will decrease and increase in a rhythmic movement. Repeat the variable-width zigzag again in a different thread weight. Simple it is, but oh, so versatile.

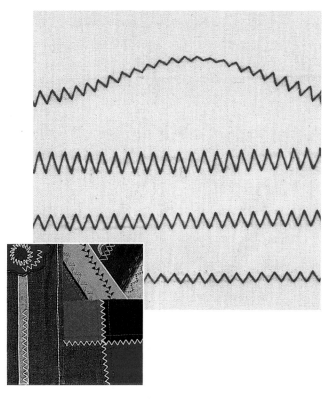

Satin stitch

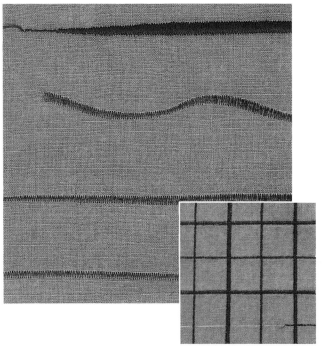

The zigzag stitches touch each other as they form a bead of thread in a vertical row. This setting is frequently used on appliqué, but it is equally interesting in a variety of independent design possibilities: sewing the stitch in rows, circles, etc. Sewn in various widths, the satin stitch can reinforce or define a softer imagery. It can strengthen two contrasting colored patches when sewn as a strong complementary colored stitch between the two units. The satin stitch can be adjusted in width from a very narrow 2-mm (or less) to a 9-mm-wide stitch, as dictated by the machine model, changing its "presence" with every increase. It is dynamic as a design stitch sewn across a patch in a soft, curved wave or in contrasting ridged stripes, or plaids with satin stitch rows criss-crossing one another.

Compact stitches

This group of stitches is sewn in solid thread segments, usually in a geometric shape. Machine choices of imagery and detail vary in style from a soft, curved scallop to the tailored boldness of a triangle or diamond. Computerized machines offer the advantage of flipping these stitches from left to right and vice versa, sewing single patterns, and expanding the pre-set millimeter size. In high-contrast color, the compact stitch is rich and dominant. Single pattern units playfully enrich a patch. For added interest, sew an outline straight stitch along the compact-stitch edge.

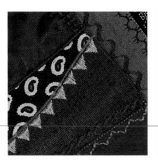 

Herringbone or cross-stitch

These units are simple machine patterns made in the form of an X. Images range from a single sequence with the X formed in a double-needle swing to a multiple group of X's in a row. Herringbone patterns can also be varied with solid satin-stitch units interspersed between the X's. Still other combinations form small dogs, flowers, and other images. All of these modifications are strong and attractive in rayon and cotton threads, and they look particularly great in the topstitch threads, sewn with a looser top tension.

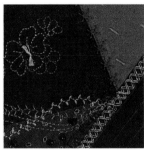

Hand-look stitches

These stitches replicate the classic hand-embroidery stitches, while offering the advantages of automatic machine alterations. This category is symbolic of the most beloved stitch styles sewn on traditional crazy quilts: the feather stitch, buttonhole, etc., all captured efficiently and creatively. Thin and shiny threads create delicate, gentle open stitches, while coarse, thick or metallic threads in the same stitch choice result in a folksy, ethnic appearance. Added dimension is found in choices of length, width, and thread. Sew hand-look stitches next to a satin stitch or give them center stage by accenting a feather row with a cluster of beads. Pushing forward, try the stitches in wide then narrow widths, changing the stitch width as you sew. I think you'll agree that hand-look stitches are invaluable. They often create the chemistry of the quilt.

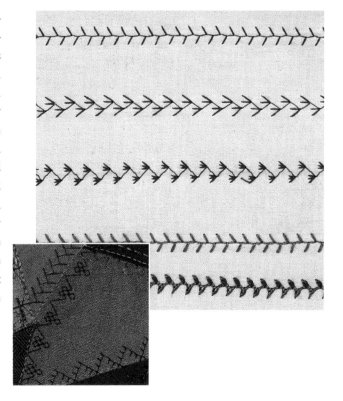

Edging stitches

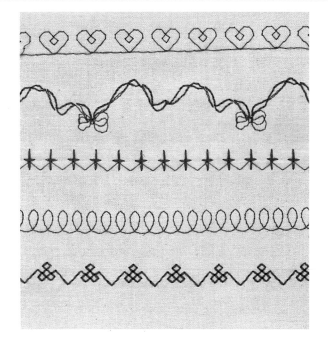

These are one-sided stitch motifs that form points, scrolls, X's, and a variety of combinations to one side of a straight stitch. Turn the patch around to sew a different direction or use the computerized mirror-image function. This stitch style looks great sewn by itself or to the edge of a contrasting satin stitch.

 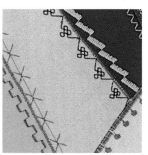

Blanket or buttonhole stitch

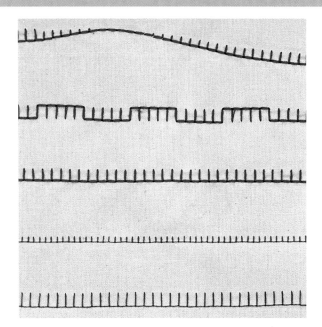

This is one of the more popular edging stitches. Sew it classic, then stretch the limit. Discover a magical strength in a row of altered length and width or multiple rows of buttonhole stitches stacked on one another. Try the stitch worked on each side of a satin stitch to create webbings, spines, or fences. Curve and intertwine two rows of buttonhole stitches. Edge-stitch an appliqué or add texture to the center of a motif. Push the classic stitch one step further with the mirror-image function or change the unit size. Consider thin or thick thread variations. Use it often and with variety.

 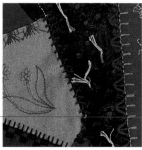

Character stitches

This multi-motion decorative stitch group produces hearts, flowers, small animals, and such. Sewn as single units or in rows, the design options vary from interesting and beautiful to playful and surprise!...occasionally, ugly. Used simply (less is more), they are enjoyable, but used around every patch, they become redundant. Sew these designs on solid or near-solid patch colors and strengthen the imagery with adjacent simple geometric or satin stitches. I recommend you use these stitches carefully. Too many joined to each other can be distracting.

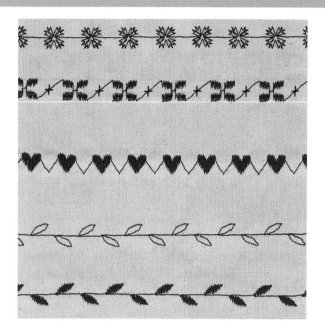

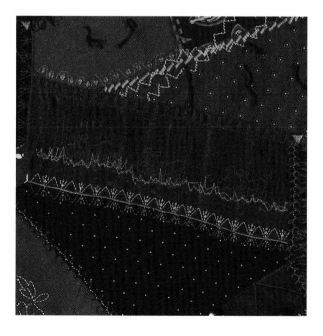

Alphabets

Many machines have available at least one alphabet font, and often more, in a width up to 9 mm. Sewn by using the computerized machine memory, the alphabet is useful for simple inscriptions, short verse, names, and such. To create an alphabet or word sequence, engage the machine memory. Follow your machine manual for specific directions. Generally, the memory is easy to use. Touch or dial a setting that opens a file on the machine, designed to record a series of letters. After opening the file, spell the name or words desired, inserting punctuation as necessary. Spell check your work, then touch the appropriate button to save the message. The message is ready to sew. Always sew a trial sample to determine the length of the words and check the thread choice. Store the selected names and sentences in the machine as long as they are useful.

Fun Quotes to Embroider

Enjoy using your machines alphabet to add your favorite sayings to your quilts. Unless credit is given, the quote is anonymous.

What you can't get out of, get into wholeheartedly.

When you don't have red, use blue.

Yesterday's the past, tomorrow's the future, today is a gift.

We make a living by what we get,
We make a life by what we give.

You can't help getting older but you don't have to get old. George Burns

Nothing great happens until after you're forty.
Coco Channel.

If you don't treat me right...shame on you!
Louis Armstrong

A good laugh is sunshine in the house.
William M. Thackeray

It's kind of fun to do the impossible. Walt Disney

Brief is life, but long is love. Alfred Lord Tennyson

Remember this quilt, it says I love you.

Every wise woman buildeth her house...
Proverbs 14:1

A man's work is from sun to sun,
but a mother's work is never done.

He who refreshes others will himself be refreshed.
Proverbs 11:25

"I thank my God every time I remember you."
Philippians 1:1

Love one another... John 3:11

Large multi-motion stitches

Consisting of florals, geometrics, animals, and monograms, these stitches range from 10 mm to 50 mm and are found on machines that have computerized functions. The machine is set to make one stitch unit and has a starting and stopping place that can be predetermined by using a locator acetate pattern sheet placed on the fabric for alignment before stitching. The machine stitch program moves the needle back and forth and sideways, creating a single image. Designs range from traditional to funny, from simple to complex. Sew the designs on separate stabilized fabric patches first, then integrate the embellished patch into the crazy-patch design. The designs are perfect for centered patchwork imagery and look great embellished with beads, buttons, etc.

Additional memory options

The sewing machine memory function allows numerous stitch choices to be placed together, then sewn as one. In essence, this gives you an entirely new directory of stitches. Simple combinations of two stitches, such as the straight and feather, look wonderful together, as does a grouping of two to three compact stitches integrated next to one another. The memory feature is usually easy to use and well worth the time to learn. It adds a creative dimension to your work.

Stacked stitch rows

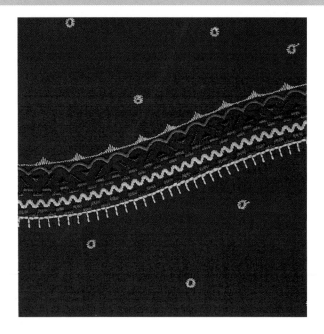

Stitches create a stronger impact when sewn in rows, edge to edge. With contrasting thread colors, sew a serpentine or other compact stitch for the center row. Add an edging stitch to each side of the compact stitch. Then, if desired, add beads or single-motif stitches outside the edging rows. Adjacent rows give "more for the money" and expand the possibilities for machine decorative stitching.

Miscellaneous stitches

These include webs, fans, and personal design choices. Some stitch choices will not be pre-programmed on the machine. Draw your design choice on a paper sheet, then needle punch the paper with an unthreaded machine needle to make a stencil. Using a pounce pad to transfer the drawn design to the crazy patch. Sew the design outline with a thick cotton thread or narrow satin stitch.

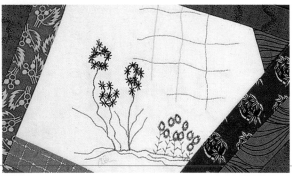

Stabilizers

The push and shove of the multi-motion needle, the contrast of softness and stiffness of fabric texture, and the unevenness of one fabric layer relative to another requires fabric preparation for maximum stitch beauty. Using one or more stabilizers is the answer to the variable components of decorative stitch sewing. Stabilizers come in many forms, and are interchangeable for different areas of the crazy patch. If you sew an open, decorative stitch across smooth cotton, perhaps no stabilizer is necessary, but if you sew the same open stitch across uneven fabric layers, you will have greater quality success if you place a strip of tear-away stabilizer or freezer paper under the foundation cloth. The stabilizer evens out the "push and shove" and engages the stitch to a more satisfactory finish. Keep available all the stabilizer choices and use them together or independently as the patch requires.

HINT

• *Cut 1" x 6" strips of a tear-away stabilizer and place them under high-stress sewing areas. Trim the stabilizer away after stitching.*

SEWING DECORATIVE STITCHES

To sew a decorative stitch, first remember that the stitches vary in complexity. The machine decorative stitches range from the simplest zigzag, with one repeat motion, to a highly complex image, such as a small dog, with movements of various lengths forward, backward, and side to side. To begin crazy-patch embellishment, select a simple, straightforward decorative stitch and sew a test fabric with several rows of sample stitch-es in different threads, tensions, widths, and lengths. Decide which is best and set your machine to repeat that style. Where fabrics of differing thicknesses are joined, the seam intersections may be very uneven. For this situation, select a simple stitch, one with few complex movements.

Then sew a decorative stitch along the patch edge:

1. Place the fabric under the needle, aligning the patch's straight stitch-appliqué line with the needle position (Fig. 7–4). To avoid fabric tunneling, center a 1" x 6" strip of stabilizer under the foundation fabric. Select the stitch and check the settings.

2. Place the needle and bobbin threads under and behind the presser foot. Position the threads in the thread holder, if your machine has one, or hold them by hand until you have sewn a couple of stitches.

3. Sew the selected stitch, keeping the presser foot evenly aligned with the patch edge. Lock the stitches at the beginning and the end.

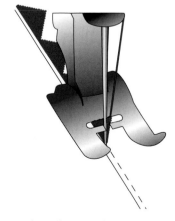

Fig. 7–4. Align the straight-stitch line with the needle.

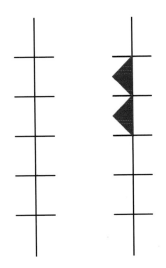

Fig. 7–5. *To align stitches,* mark where each pattern begins.

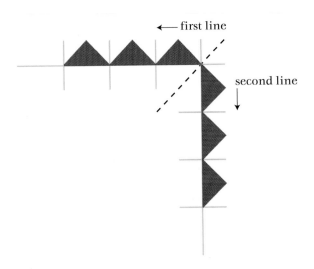

first line ⟵

second line ↓

Fig. 7–6. *To sew a corner,* sew in the direction of the arrows.

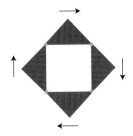

Fig. 7–7. *For symmetrical shapes,* with needle down, turn 90 degrees. The needle-down positions are shown in blue.

HINT

• *To lock stitches, you can backstitch two to three stitches. Use the machine's auto-lock feature, or sew in place two to three stitches.*

If the row ends in a partial pattern, the ending will be covered by the stitches sewn down the adjacent side. If the stitch ending image is important, then carefully finish it with a complete stitch cycle or sew a straight stitch the last half inch to avoid conflicting with the first row.

Aligning two stitches. With a fine-point fabric marking pencil, mark a horizontal line at the exact location where each of the patterns begins (Fig. 7–5).

For a manual machine, sew the decorative stitch down the patch edge. When the pattern finishes, stop, bring the needle up, and set the needle to the adjacent side, inserting the needle on the horizontal pencil line. Be sure the stitch is at the beginning of its cycle.

A computerized machine will automatically begin the stitch pattern at the beginning of the stitch cycle. If the stitch was stopped in the middle of a cycle, touch the pattern-begin button. Align the needle with the adjacent side, inserting the needle on the horizontal pencil line.

Sew a corner.

Easy method – To make a sample, sew a decorative stitch from the corner downward. Remove the fabric from the needle and turn it. Reset the decorative stitch to the beginning position and sew the second side of the corner (Fig. 7–6).

Continuous method – Sew a test sample of two to three repeats of a pattern. Measure the distance of the repeat, then mark the

Sew Crazy with Decorative Threads & Stitches – *Alice Kolb*

repeat distance on a piece of fabric. Sew from mark to mark, watching the pattern fill the space. If you can see that the pattern will be slightly off as you approach the second mark, you can feed in more or less fabric or you can increase or decrease the stitch length slightly so the pattern ends exactly at the second mark. At a corner, stop at the end of the pattern with the needle inserted in the fabric, pivot, and continue.

Border turn. This stitch style is particularly suited to the computerized machine. Set the computerized function of one stitch pattern. Sew one pattern, pause with needle in the fabric, and turn the fabric. By turning left or right, squares, circles, and horizontal rows can be designed (Fig. 7–7).

HINT
- *With fabric marking pencil, draw the square, circle, or linear background lines. Use them as guides to pivot the correct degree.*

Double-needle. Insert a double needle in the machine. Follow the machine's manual to place two spools of decorative thread on the top spindles. Thread the bobbin with a blending thread color. Set the stitch width so the needle swing is inside the presser foot opening to avoid breaking the needle. Select an open-styled decorative stitch and sew, doubling the effect (Fig. 7–8). Avoid complex multi-motion stitches.

Ribbon edge. Select edging stitches to enhance grosgrain ribbons (Fig. 7–9). Set the stitch one-eighth inch inside the ribbon edge and sew. Use a stabilizer under ribbon, if necessary. Attach decorated ribbon to the patchwork with a straight stitch or fusing strip.

Fig. 7–8. Double-needle possibilities.

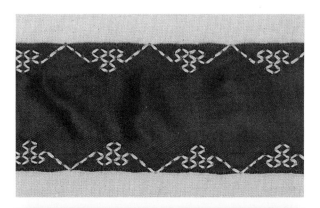

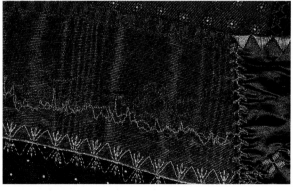

Fig. 7–9. Edge stitches on ribbon.

TIPS FOR TROUBLES

Stitch Attitude. At first, stitch "attitude" may seem humorous, but all the components of the stitch do indeed create an attitude. The stitch choice, the thread, the tension setting, the width and length, and the placement of one stitch relative to another set the tone for charm or tangle, for excitement or frustration. If you are unhappy with the result of a stitch row, critique the following variables and make the necessary changes.

Starting and stopping. The components of a stitch involve several variables, the control of which will make the stitch easier to sew. Use the presser foot that makes the stitch most easily seen. Usually the open-toed embroidery foot is a good choice. Be sure to lock the beginning and ending of the stitch line. To prevent the fabric seam from "growing" as you stitch, start embellishing the patches from the center of the quilt and move outward as the work advances.

Uneven fabric thicknesses. If your patchwork has a variety of fabric weights, you will need to find ways to manage the uneven seams and the problems they cause, such as uneven stitches, pleats in the fabric, fabric caught in the feed dogs, and the feed system immobilized by excessive thickness. Create a solution by inserting a strip of stabilizer under the seam to aid in stitch travel and selecting an open-styled stitch to sew over uneven areas.

HINT

• *Press the bulky fabric's edges flat before placing a lighter-weight fabric on top.*

Stitch doesn't show. Select a stitch that has more thread structure or select a thread with higher color contrast. You could also use a compact stitch or topstitch, or choose metallic thread. Try "overstitching" the first stitch run or use a contrasting thread color and sew adjacent to the first stitch, in a curved or chevron pattern.

HINT

• *Separate busy prints with solid-colored fabrics. The stitches will show more vividly.*

Bunching stitches. If the stitch is sewing unevenly, try changing to an open, airy stitch. Place a stabilizer strip under the foundation fabric. Re-sew the patch from the other end, reaching the problem area last.

Poor stitch quality. Clean your machine and change the needle. Add another strip of stabilizer and loosen the stitch length and top tension. Select the needle-down feature to keep the needle in the fabric when you stop and reposition the fabric or yourself.

Reverse sewing. Need to take stitches out? With small scissors, clip embroidery threads on the back of the fabric. Pull and discard the loose threads, working gently from front and back. Repeat the clip-and-pull procedure until all the threads have been removed. A long, thin needle or thin, sharp seam ripper is helpful for inserting under the thread roll to pull one thread at a time.

EXPLORING DECORATIVE STITCHES

To customize a stitch, sew it in an assortment of widths, lengths, and threads (Figs. 7–10a and b). With a permanent ink pen, record the stitch setting on the fabric piece. Keep the labeled pieces as a permanent record of your experiments. Transfer your favorite stitches to the project patches.

Make a Sample

First, cut a 3" x 6" strip of solid-colored, interfaced cotton. Then...

1. Select a stitch and sew it exactly as it is pre-set in the sewing machine.

2. Sew the same stitch with an adjusted width, increased or decreased by at least one number.

3. Sew the same stitch with an adjusted length, by at least one number.

4. Sew the same stitch with both width and length adjusted.

5. Sew several rows of the stitch: straight rows, curved rows, crossed rows (plaid).

6. Sew a narrow satin stitch next to an adjusted decorative stitch row.

7. Sew the stitch in mirror image.

8. Combine the mirror image in memory with another stitch.

9. Sew expanded units, if your machine has this feature.

MANAGING STITCH QUALITY

With every stitch, there is only one goal, to sew a fine stitch, in essence, to sew a stitch row that enhances the project. From a selection of thread color and decorative stitches, it is a good idea to quickly sew what I refer to as "my insurance policy." I sew a sample row of the stitch, changing the tension as I go, then check the stitch quality. This quickly determines the most attractive stitch setting and quality and prevents redo's on the project.

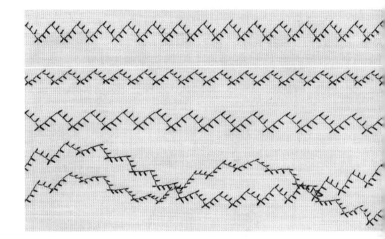

Fig. 7–10a. Exploring a feather stitch, top to bottom: standard, reduced, expanded, crooked, altered.

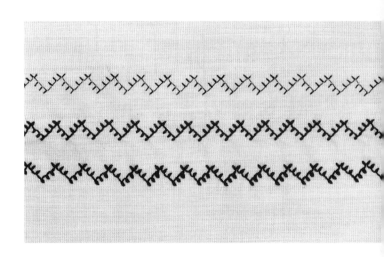

Fig. 7–10b. Exploring a feather stitch, top to bottom: silk finish cotton thread, top-stitched thread, perle rayon from the bobbin.

Make a Sample

1. Cut an actual project fabric "mock-up," including the muslin foundation, patch fabric, and stabilizer to be used. Sew the patch fabric with its stabilizer on a muslin strip 3" x 10".

2. Place the appropriate needle, the needle thread, and the bobbin thread in a clean machine.

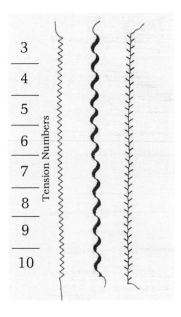

Fig. 7–11. Stitch quality test.

3. Draw horizontal lines across the 10" strip at 1" intervals. Number the vertical edge of the strip with the needle tension numbers 3–10 along the intervals.

4. With the strip under the presser foot, sew a row of the selected decorative stitch, changing the needle tension disc number as you sew to match the marked numbers in each interval.

5. At the end of the stitch row, critique the stitches for the best quality. Use that tension setting for your project (Fig. 7–11).

FINE TUNING

With the variable choices of threads and fabric, a stitch adjustment is often necessary to balance the differences in thread thickness and fabric weight.

Normal tension. This setting secures the needle and bobbin thread in the fabric in an even proportion. It is often marked with a bold line on the tension knob.

Loosen tension. Dial one or more numbers lower (smaller number) to enhance the thread beauty of decorative stitches. This lower tension is useful with the satin stitch setting.

Tighten tension. Dial one or two numbers higher (larger number) than normal, which forces the needle thread to stay on the surface and pulls the bobbin thread upward. Use with top-stitching threads.

Length adjustment. The stitch-length dial controls how open or closed each thread cycle is; for example, how close zigzag stitches set together.

Width adjustment. The stitch-width dial controls how narrow or wide each stitch is.

Fig. 7–12. Appliquéd and embroidered horse.

Appliqué Embellishments

A complementary addition to crazy stitching is the ornamentation known as appliqué (Fig. 7–12). Well-known and loved in its own right, the contrast of one fabric accent applied to another is a welcome addition, whether sewn in the center of a patch or as one component of a patchwork block.

Bits of contrasting fabric; a simple design, such as a flower, house, bird, or geometric shape; and an attractive edging stitch are the beginnings of interesting appliqué. For the greatest appliqué impact on crazy stitching, select high-contrast complementary colors in the appliqué fabrics. Then consider a blending thread (for example, a red thread on a red flower) to sew the appliqué to the background, or take a bolder approach and sew a high-contrast thread color around the shape (for example, a red thread on a blue flower).

HINT

• *Some fabrics sew better if a stabilizer is used under the background fabric. Freezer paper can also be used. Tear away the freezer paper or stabilizer after the sewing has been completed.*

TYPES OF APPLIQUÉ

Select fabric textures and colors for each part of the appliqué design. Prewash the fabrics, if desired, to prevent fading and puckering. Cut squares equal to the largest appliqué shape plus one inch.

To transfer the patterns to the squares, trace the designs on the paper side of a fusible web. Remember to reverse asymmetrical shapes. Fuse the web to the wrong side of the fabrics. Cut shapes on the pencil line. Peel the paper away. Place each appliqué on the background. Fuse the appliqués to the background, following the the fusible web directions.

Supplies

- Appliqué design
- Fabrics for each appliqué section and background fabric
- Zigzag sewing machine with open-toed embroidery foot
- Foundation fabrics: paper-backed fusible web, removable pull-away stabilizer, or freezer paper
- Threads appropriate to the color and appliqué image
- General sewing supplies: scissors, pencil, ruler, etc.

Appliqué Thread Choices

Fine Threads

Extra-fine cotton—machine embroidery
Rayon
Bobbin thread for thin threads—cotton 60 wgt.
   Bobbin-fil, matched to needle thread

Medium Threads

Metallic
Top-stitch thread
Bobbin thread for medium threads—Polyester, Metrolene by Mettler

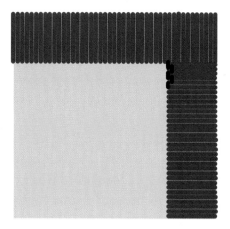

Fig. 7–13. Sew across the end of the satin stitch to lock the threads.

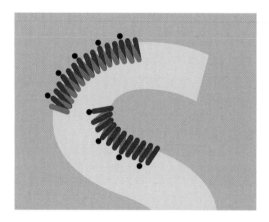

Fig. 7–14. Pivot points for an outside and for an inside curve.

Fig. 7–15. Appliquéd outside and inside curves.

Satin-stitch appliqué. Thread and needle choices are critical to the successful appearance of satin-stitch appliqué. Select fine thread for the needle and matching or lighter-weight thread for bobbin.

> **MACHINE SETTINGS**
> Width, zigzag to 2½
> Length, satin stitch
> Top tension, normal to one or
>   two smaller numbers
> Bobbin tension, balanced

Sewing

1. Begin appliquéing by sewing at an inside detail. First, lower the needle into the cloth and lock the threads by sewing a straight stitch forward two to three short stitches.

2. Set the machine to the satin-stitch. Lift the presser foot and return to the beginning of the pattern. Sew the satin stitch around an appliqué. (Set the stitch to touch the outside edge of the appliqué unit.) To end the satin stitch, sew a straight stitch two or three stitches across the end of the stitch (Fig. 7–13). If the thread is slippery, pull the needle thread to the back and tie it.

HINTS

• *To examine a thread color's compatibility with a fabric, hold a spool of thread sideways to the appliqué fabric. Look at the total thread spool color, not just one strand. Make a decision based on the way the color reads, whether it's an exact match or a contrast pleasing to the appliqué and background fabric.*

• *A slightly looser top tension creates a prettier satin stitch because the thread coverage will be fuller. The looser tension also helps keep the bobbin thread from showing.*

• *For an outside curve, sew with the stitches in*

the background fabric just outside the appliqué edge. The needle swing should just touch the appliqué edge (Fig. 7–14). At the end of the curve, stop with the needle in the background fabric.

• For an inside curve, sew as for an outside curve, stopping the needle swing on the edge of the appliqué shape (Fig. 7–14 and Fig. 7–15).

• There are two ways to turn a corner with a line of satin stitching. For the straight-stitch turn, sew to the end of the corner, ending with the needle down on the outside of the corner. Pivot and switch to a straight stitch for two or three stitches, then return to the satin stitch and continue sewing (Fig. 7–16). For the zigzag turn, after ending with the needle in the outside corner, lengthen the zigzag so that taking one zigzag stitch will put the needle down on the other side of the satin stitch. Return to the satin stitch and continue sewing (Fig. 7–17).

Edge-stitched appliqué. Sewing appliqué edges with the buttonhole stitch or a simple cross-stitch is very effective when sewn with a bold thread, such as a topstitch thread. A casual, homey, or ethnic-style appearance results. Select the thread, needle, and tension settings to match the fabric (see page 64). If you are a beginner, use this stitch for round, oval, or straight shapes, not petal shapes.

MACHINE SETTINGS
Width, 2½–5
Length, 3½–6
Top tension, normal or higher
Bobbin tension, balanced for strong thread

Sewing

1. Set the stitch to swing to the left — toward the body of the appliqué patch.

2. To secure the stitch, begin by lowering the needle into the background and sewing one or two straight stitches.

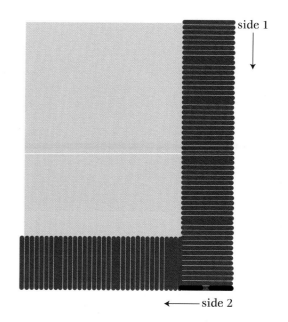

Fig. 7–16. Straight-stitch turn.

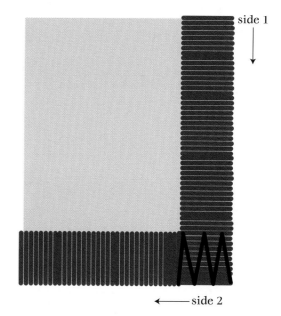

Fig. 7–17. Zigzag turn.

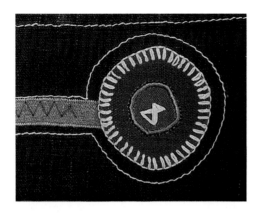

Fig. 7–18. The straight edge of the buttonhole stitch is made in the background fabric.

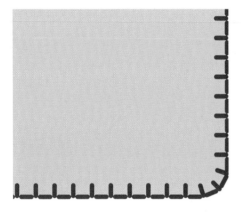

Fig. 7–19. Turn corners gradually.

Fig. 7–20. Meander quilting.

3. Select the buttonhole stitch and set it to the desired width. Pull the threads up and behind the presser foot. Begin sewing, guiding the straight edge of the buttonhole stitch along the cut edge of the appliqué (Fig. 7–18).

4. For curves, stop with the needle in the appliqué. You will want to turn corners gradually and reduce the stitch length. Take a few stitches and stop. Lift the presser foot and pivot the piece. Lower the presser foot and take a few more stitches (Fig. 7–19). The left-swing thread points should touch but not overlap. The tighter the curve, the more frequently you will need to pivot. For each curve, do a trial run and count the number of stitches between pivots. Repeat this "count and turn" to get a good result. For interest, sew the stitch so the decorative edge falls to the outside of the appliqué.

5. End the stitch by turning the stitch dial back to the straight stitch and take one more stitch. Leave a thread tail.

6. Pull the beginning and ending thread tails to the back. Tie the threads together, snugging them to the fabric, and hand knot.

Free-motion Embroidery

A third style of stitch embellishment suited to machine crazy patch is free-motion stitching. Typically used for meandering or stippling in machine quilting (Fig. 7–20), the design effects are unlimited. The stitch can be purely spontaneous and free in spirit, or it can follow a tracing to achieve an exact image. Stitch movement, pattern, and choice of thread dictate the end result (Fig. 7–21).

Supplies

- Chalk fabric pencil
- Zigzag sewing machine with free-motion embroidery foot
- 5"–8" machine embroidery hoop (optional)
- Foundation fabric: tear-away stabilizer
- Thread color appropriate for the image.

Thread Choices for Appliqué

Fine Threads

Extra-fine cotton-machine embroidery

Rayon

Bobbin: thin all-purpose, matched to the needle thread.

Medium Threads

Metallic

Top-stitch

Bobbin: Mettler Metrolene polyester to match the needle thread.

HINT

- *Medium threads are best used for a folk-art or ethnic look. Perfection is difficult to achieve in free-motion with thicker threads.*

Needle Choices for Appliqué

Match needle to bobbin thread and decorative thread, see Recipe Cards, pages 64 – 65.

Sewing

1. *Optional:* Use fabric chalk pencil or a pounce pad to transfer a specific design to stabilized fabric.
2. Stretch the fabric taut in an embroidery hoop. Position the hoop in the machine so that the fabric rests on the sewing table under the presser foot (Fig. 7–22).
3. Support the fabric with your hands on each side of the hoop in a "C" position, in which the thumb and index fingers are

Free-motion Embroidery Ideas

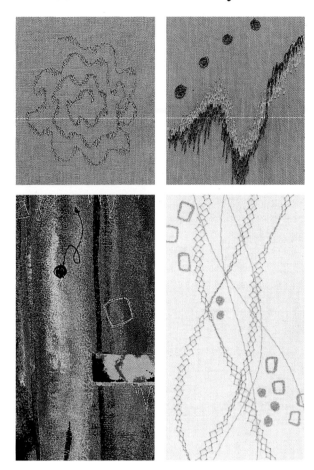

Fig. 7–21. Spontaneous stitching.

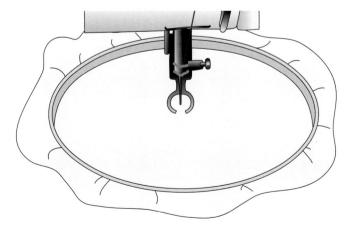

Fig. 7–22. The fabric rests on the sewing table.

Supplies

- Needle: top-stitch needle with medium-weight thread, such as a polyester or a top-stitch thread
- Bobbin: medium to coarse-weight thread with a metallic look, top-stitch weight, or ribbon appearance
- Zigzag sewing machine with embroidery open-toed foot
- Extra bobbin case
- Chalk fabric marking pencil
- Stabilized fabric patch

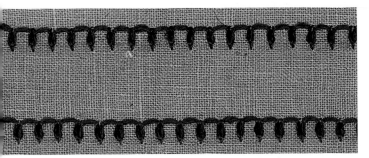

Fig. 7–23. Bobbin thread embroidery. (a) Balanced needle and bobbin tension. (b) Skew top tension tight and bobbin tension loose to achieve both colors.

Bobbin thread embroidery.

shaped into the letter "C". Begin by securing threads by stitching one or two times in place. Starting on a fairly straight side, rather than at a point or "V," create designs as you sew, or sew around a traced design. Move the hoop slowly and evenly. Keep the motor speed even.

4. At the end of the design, stop and secure threads as before or, if heavier thread is used, pull both threads to back and tie.

Bobbin Thread Embroidery

Many threads are available that are too thick, too wiry, or too soft for traditional needle sewing. Sewing these threads from a bobbin has exciting advantages because you can expand the number of different types of thread used, and with variable machine adjustments, you can create a hand-look of thicker threads or two thread colors showing in one stitch (Fig. 7–23). For more bobbin stitches, see the larger photo on page 124.

HINT
- As a general rule, if the cut end of the thread looks like a paintbrush, sew from the bobbin.

To begin decorative bobbin thread sewing, purchase an alternate bobbin case and adjust its tension for the thicker thread. Keep the original bobbin case adjusted for general sewing. With two cases, you can easily switch back and forth and save time adjusting the bobbin case. If possible, when you purchase your extra bobbin case, have your machine mechanic loosen and adjust the bobbin screw for thicker thread sewing. Then it will be easy to make minor adjustments, as needed.

Because the bobbin tension screw is very short, it must be adjusted in small increments. To adjust the bobbin, loosen the tension screw if you want the thread to pull through more quickly and tighten the screw if you want the thread to feed more slowly. First observe the position of the slot in the head of the screw. Give the slot a "clock time." From that time, adjust left or right, not to exceed "15 minutes." Remember, the tension screw is very short. The time position will help you remember what the original setting was.

My favorite word to use with bobbin thread sewing is "experiment." After all bobbin adjustments have been made, sew a row and check the stitch image. Adjust the bobbin tension looser or tighter, if necessary, to get the desired result.

HINT

• *Sewing machine screws work like any other screw. Turn clockwise to tighten and counter-clockwise to loosen. Remember, "lefty-loosey, righty-tighty."*

From a variety of novelty threads, select Cordonnet, #8 perle cotton, a wiry metallic, or narrow ribbon to fill the bobbin. Because these threads are thicker, the bobbin will hold less thread. Plan to wind several bobbins at once to save time and avoid the inconvenience of rewinding in the middle of a project. If the thread is on a spindle, wind it in the normal fashion. If it is wound in a ball, place the ball in a cup to keep it in control, then thread it to the bobbin winder. Wind the thread on the bobbin slowly and evenly, filling to within a fingernail's thickness of the edge of the bobbin.

To sew, first check the stitch quality by making the following sample.

1. Use a top-stitch needle with medium-weight thread if you want the top thread to show too; if not, select a matching color in polyester for the needle thread.

2. Cut a stabilized fabric strip. Mark the tension numbers along the edge of back of the strip in one-inch intervals.
3. Select an open-styled stitch (zigzag or hand-look). Set the stitch width at medium (4–5) and the stitch length as desired.
4. Turn the patch right side down and sew, changing the top tension to correspond to the one-inch intervals.
5. Turn the fabric right side up and select the nicest stitch tension from the sample.
6. Set the machine to the selected top tension, often a higher number. Loosen the bobbin tension and sew the desired pattern on the crazy-patch fabric.

HINTS

• *Draw a sewing guide line on the back of the patch.*
• *Place the fabric under the presser foot, then pull the bobbin thread up to fabric's surface to avoid tangles on the underside (Fig. 7–24).*
• *The back side of the straight-stitch appliqué line is a perfect guide for bobbin thread sewing.*

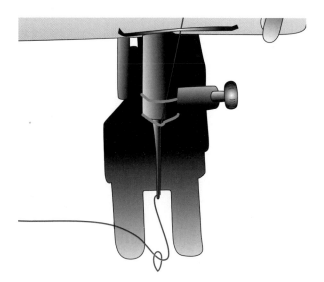

Fig. 7–24. Pull the bobbin thread to the top.

Seam Embroidery

Interesting as each stitch is, combining the various stitches explodes the possibilities for design. Integrating stitch styles requires visual and technical choices. This section focuses on the decorative seam stitches, that is, the stitches that run down the seam line between two patches. Individual patches are embellished with centered machine embroidery motifs long before the seam embellishments are made, yet the seam decorative work shouts "Wow!" Each seam's accent links the patches together, creating a continuous flow of color and stitches. The decorative seam embroidery can take charge with its boldness of color or thread stroke, or it can fall quietly into the patch. Each stitch row creates an action line by the manner in which it is sewn on the patchwork.

There are two methods of applying seam decorative stitches:

1. Sew a decorative stitch down the center of a seam between patches (Fig. 7–25).

Fig. 7–25. Using several decorative stitches with beads.

2. Sew a decorative stitch down each patch edge, then insert a filler, usually a satin stitch, between the two decorative stitches.

Both of these methods are successful and can be used interchangeably across a project. The use of both styles in the same project creates a bold accent, adding interest to the piece. A third accent may be considered. Beads and small buttons stitched to each stitch point or curve will expand the stitch width, visually enhance the color, add movement to the stitch, and reinforce the stitch imagery. Add beads after stitching.

Sew multiple rows. Sew a row of stitches down the edge of a patch. Repeat a second row on the adjacent patch. Then, setting the machine to a narrow width and contrasting thread color, satin stitch a narrow line down the center of the two rows of stitches (see page 67).

Create a "dance line." Set the machine on a wide, open-styled stitch and use a medium-weight thread. Use chalk to draw lines to follow, or free-hand sew, your dance line (a wavy line, see page 37) across one or two patches or, occasionally, to create an even longer line. The high-contrast wavy line is dramatic and adds high energy to your piece.

EXPERIMENT

- Use a decorative top-stitch thread in the needle and the bobbin to sew a line of embroidery stitches along a seam. Skew the tension so both threads show.
- Use thick-and-thin thread in the needle, creating two rows of stitches, side by side.
- Sew a line of stitches with a compact thread, then outline it with a thin straight line.
- Sew a crooked line for a short distance, followed by a straight line. Continue alternating crooked and straight lines.

Beading

Accent beads provide a strong design force on crazy quilts. They strengthen a row of zigzag stitches, add magic when sewn around a button, and pull a dull, ordinary motif into play. Add beads by hand when you have finished the machine embellishment.

Supplies

- Beading needle or #10–12 hand-quilting needle
- Beading thread: clear in taupe, black, or white (blend color with bead and fabric)
- Glass beads
- Old beads

BEAD CLUSTERS

1. Work with a thread length of 15"–18".
2. Secure the thread tails in the fabric.
3. Thread one bead and pull it snug to the fabric, concealing the lock stitch.
4. Repeat for each bead in the cluster. Tie a knot to end, then pull the threads under the fabric.

ROWS OF BEADS

1. Sew one bead snug to fabric, then thread a second bead on the needle.
2. Insert the needle down next to first bead, sewing a series of cursive "e's" (Fig. 7–26).
3. Keep the travel distance between ½" to 1".
4. Secure the threads by pulling a knot under the fabric. Trim the threads.

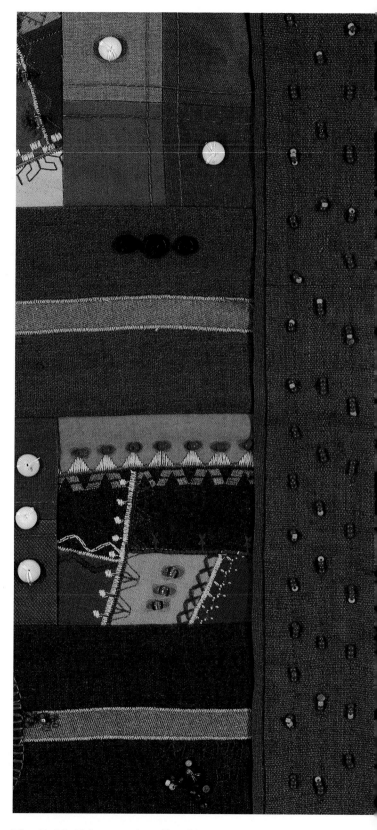

Fig. 7–26. Using a series of beads.

Chapter 8

Finishing the Work

Sew Crazy with Decorative Threads & Stitches – *Alice Kolb*

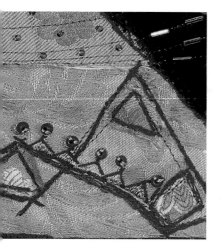

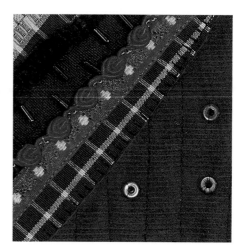

Webster tells us the word "finish" means "to bring to an end." Crazy patch is finished, I suppose, when you stop stitching, because there is always the consideration of one more row, one more button, and one more detail. I make this decision when I can honestly look at each block and feel satisfied with the embellishment. It is a feeling of satisfaction, of completeness, a time to move to the next step. This chapter covers several finishing processes suited to the different quilt styles, along with binding and labeling information for your project.

With All My Heart, 17" x 18"

made by Fran Patterson, Austin, Texas.

WITH ALL MY HEART is a delightful collage of vintage fabrics patched and embellished in a stylized heart motif.

Joining Blocks

1. Pull stray threads to the back. Tie and trim them. Clean your quilt blocks by folding a strip of masking tape sticky side out. Use it to remove thread tags and lint.

2. Lightly press your blocks in selected areas. Press carefully and gingerly. Use low heat and a pressing cloth, such as a piece of muslin, or a soft towel if the embellishment has depth. Never slide the iron across the block, but instead, smooth and freshen areas of the block. Always read the heat setting before touching the fabric.

3. Square the blocks as follows: Lay out all the blocks on a flat surface and determine which is the smallest one. Place each individual block on a grid-style cutting mat and, using a rotary cutter, trim each block to the desired finished size plus ½" (¼" seam allowance on each side). Always check the measurements with the first block. Check to be sure you are leaving an adequate seam allowance usually ¼" beyond any points (intersection of two seams) at the outside edges of the blocks.

4. Plan the block arrangement. With each block cut and pressed, place the blocks side by side. Look at the grouping and rearrange them as necessary to create the best color placement.

5. Decide on a quilt setting and sew the blocks together to create your preferred style. All seam allowances are ¼".

Finishing the Various Quilt Styles

The following information may be useful for specific quilt styles (see pages 25 and 26).

Whole-cloth. Secure the quilt top to a flat surface, ideally one with a cutting grid. Straighten one long side and one short side. Use masking tape to secure the quilt to the cutting surface. Carefully measure the cut sides and use these measurements to cut the remaining sides.

Patchwork tiles. Sew the blocks together, creating rows. Then sew the rows together, taking care to match each intersecting seam. Press as you go.

Sashing. Use the following information to cut sashing strips of lightly interfaced fabric to sew between patchwork blocks (Fig. 8–1).

Cut vertical sashes the same length as the block size including seam allowances. Sew the sashes in between the blocks for each row.

For the horizontal sashes, measure the length of the sewn rows, including the vertical sashing strips. Cut the horizontal sashes

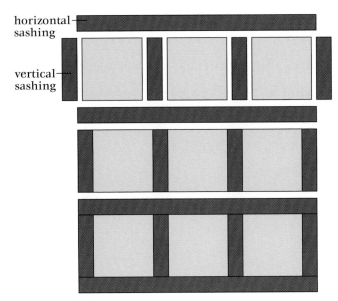

horizontal sashing

vertical sashing

Fig. 8–1. Adding sashing strips.

the length of an average row, including seam allowances. Sew the horizontal sashes between the block rows. Press each seam and press the whole quilt top lightly.

On-point.

1. Cut squares of plain fabric to equal the size of the crazy-patch squares. Cut triangle shapes (setting pieces) to fill in the sides and corners of the quilt to make it square.
2. Sew the crazy-patch blocks to the plain squares, alternating them checkerboard fashion to make a row.
3. Make multiple rows to complete the desired size of quilt. Press each seam.
4. Place the rows on the diagonal (on-point) and complete each row with setting triangles (Fig. 8–2).

   Side triangles – Using the finished block size, multiply by 1.414 and add 1¼" to find the size of square needed. Cut the square twice diagonally to create four side triangles.

   Corner triangles – Using the finished block size, divide by 1.414 and add ⅞" to find the size of square needed. Cut the square once diagonally to produce two corner triangles.

5. Sew the diagonal rows together, carefully matching each intersection.

Medallion. Decide how wide you want your borders to be. To find the length to cut, add twice the border width to the measured quilt length and add another 2" for seam allowances and insurance. Cut the the border strips the desired width plus ½" for seam allowances.

Select the Log Cabin or Courthouse Steps style of application:

Log Cabin – Sew border strips around the medallion center block, moving in a clockwise or counterclockwise direction. Press seam allowances toward the border strips (Fig. 8–3).

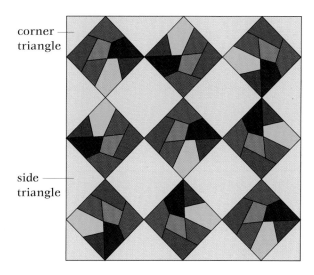

corner triangle

side triangle

Fig. 8–2. Add setting triangles to on-point blocks.

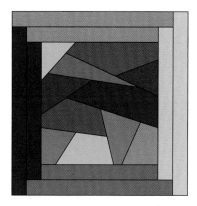

Fig. 8–3. Log Cabin-style borders.

Courthouse Steps – Sew border strips across the top and bottom of the medallion center block. Then sew strips to the left and right sides of the block. Press seam allowances toward the border strips (Fig. 8–4).

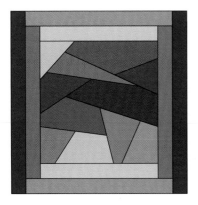

Fig. 8–4. Courthouse Steps-style borders.

Fig. 8–5. Overlap the insertion strips at the corners.

Insertion Strips

An insertion strip is a narrow folded fabric strip, usually in a strongly contrasting color, inserted between the quilt body and the border. The folded edge overlaps the patched quilt body slightly, complimenting the border and decorative blocks. An insertion is an ideal way to add pizzazz to a quilt or draw the eye toward a color.

1. Cut four straight-grain strips 1" wide and the length of the quilt body plus 2".
2. Press each strip in half lengthwise, making four ½"-wide strips.
3. Align the cut edges of strips with the raw edges of the quilt top.
4. Sew strips to opposite side of the quilt with a ¼" seam allowance. Then sew strips to the two remaining sides of the quilt to complete the insertion (Fig. 8–5).
5. Pin and sew border strips to the crazy-patch block, using the insertion strip seam as a guide.

Thin Batting

Traditionally, crazy quilts were made in two layers, an embellished quilt top and a backing fabric, tied together with simple string or floss. Batting was rarely used, but modern batts are high quality and available in a variety of thicknesses. I encourage you to consider using a thin batt to enhance your quilt.

Through the process of making the crazy-patch projects for this book, I found adding borders to the edge of a squared patchwork quilt top and sewing through a thin batt to be a successful and secure way to maintain the squareness of a quilt.

If you want to try this method, purchase the thinnest, low-loft batt you can find. Then follow these instructions:

1. Cut the batting to size, which is the size of the quilt top, including the border strips you will be adding, plus 4" more in width and length. The extra inches will help in layering. After the borders have been added and the quilt top squared, the extra inches will be cut away.

2. Place the batting on a flat surface, large enough to span the full width and length of the patchwork. Using builder's masking tape, tape the batt to the flat surface.

3. To neaten the quilt top's underside, trim and tie any hanging threads and pull or cut away excess stabilizer. This is your last chance! Once the patchwork is secured to the batting, it is much more difficult to tidy up.

4. Place the squared crazy-patch quilt top in the center of the batt (Fig. 8–6). Measure from the edge of the batt to the edge of the quilt top to ensure that the amount of batt showing is uniform on all four sides. Sew ¼" from the edge of the quilt top all around to attach it to the batt.

5. Add insertion strips, if desired.

6. Pin border strips to the cut edges of quilt, right sides together. Use a ¼" seam allowance to attach the border strips, sewing through the quilt top and the batting. Repeat for each round of borders (Fig. 8–7).

HINT

• *To sew perfectly straight insertion strips, turn the quilt over and sew down the stitching line that secures the quilt top to the batting.*

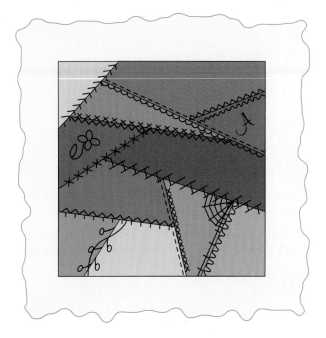

Fig. 8–6. Center the quilt top on the batting.

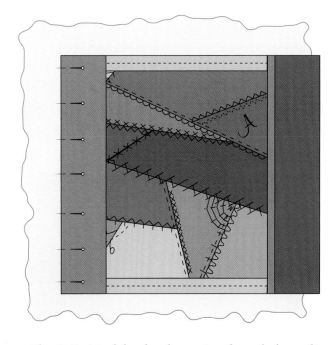

Fig. 8–7. Attach borders by sewing through the quilt top and batting.

Sign It Your Way

There are countless ways to identify and sign your quilt, but my favorite way is with a personalized bound label.

1. Sign a small interfaced rectangle of fabric from the project. Remember to include your name, date, and the title of the piece. Use the machine alphabet, cross stitch, or hand embroidery.

2. Embellish the rectangle in a style complementary to the finished quilt.

3. Cut a 1½" straight-grain or bias binding strip. Starting on a long side of the rectangle, align the edge of the strip with a edge of the label, right sides together.

4. Sew the binding to the label, ½" from edge. Add the next strip, moving in a clockwise direction. At each corner, fold in ½" of the beginning end of the binding (Fig. 8–8).

5. When all the sides have been bound, turn the binding to the back and press. Secure the back of the binding by stitching in the ditch of the seam line from the front of the piece.

6. Attach the bound label to the back of the quilt.

Layering

1. Lightly press the finished quilt top. Use masking tape to secure the quilt top to a flat surface, ideally one with a cutting grid. Use a rotary cutter and ruler to straighten one long side and one short side. Carefully measure the cut sides and use these measurements to cut the remaining sides.

2. Remove the quilt top from the flat surface. Cut a backing fabric the width of finished quilt top plus 4". Tape the backing to the flat surface.

3. Center the quilt top (with batting, if used) on the backing.

4. Pin or hand baste the sandwich unit together, securing from the center outward.

5. Tie the quilt in a way that enhances the style.

Fig. 8–8. Bind the label before sewing it to the backing.

Tying the Quilt

Tying is a classic and simple way to secure the quilt sandwich.

1. Pin-baste the quilt top, batting, and backing together.

2. Select a medium-weight thread or yarn, such as perle cotton, embroidery floss, or sport yarn, and thread it through a large-eyed tapestry needle. Do not tie the thread end.

3. Use a chalk pencil or other removable marker to mark the quilt top in a grid for tying. A 5" grid is a good size. You need mark only the grid intersections.

4. Take a stitch at the first mark and go through all three layers, carefully catching the backing, batt, and quilt top. Leave about a 3" tail, then drag the thread to the next marking, leaving a loose length. After completing a row, cut the threads in the middle between the stitches (Fig. 8–9). Secure each tie in a square knot, then trim the thread tails, leaving about 1" to create an attractive, decorative tassel (Fig. 8–10).

HINT

- *After tying, check the quilt top to see if it is square. Adjust by trimming, if necessary. Sewing through all thicknesses, secure the quilt edges with a straight stitch or narrow zigzag. Be sure to sew within the seam allowance. Securing the edges simplifies the final step, adding the binding. The backing and batting will be trimmed after the binding is applied.*

Fig. 8–9. Cut threads in between the stitches.

Fig. 8–10. Trim ties to leave a tassel.

Finish with a Binding

For this binding method, you will need to create a continuous strip that is equivalent to the perimeter of your quilt plus 12" for turning corners and joining the ends.

1. Cut strips of fabric 2½" wide, selvage to selvage.
2. Sew the strips end to end with a diagonal seam (Fig. 8–11). Trim the excess fabric from the seam allowances (Fig. 8–12). Press the seam allowances open (Fig. 8–13). Fold the continuous strip in half lengthwise (Fig. 8–14).

3. Starting on one side of the quilt, not at a corner, align the raw edges of the binding strip with the raw edge of the quilt top.
4. Leaving a tail of 8"–10" hanging free, sew the binding to quilt with a ¼" seam allowance. Stop ¼" from the corner.
5. With the needle down in the fabric, turn the quilt as if you were getting ready to sew the next side, then backstitch off the quilt edge (Fig. 8–15). Cut the threads and remove the quilt from the machine.
6. Fold the binding up at a 45-degree angle (Fig. 8–16). Fold it back down, aligning it

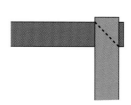

Fig. 8–11. Sew the ends together diagonally.

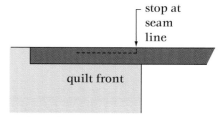

stop at
seam
line

quilt front

Backstitch to secure stitches.

Fig. 8–15. Stop ¼" from the corner and backstitch off the quilt edge.

Fig. 8–12. Trim, leaving seam allowance.

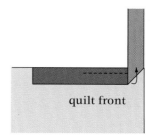

quilt front

Fig. 8–16. Fold binding up.

Fig. 8–13. Press seam allowances open.

fold

quilt front

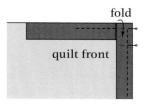

Fig. 8–14. Fold the long strip in half.

Fig. 8–17. Fold binding back down and stitch.

with the raw edges of the second side, ready to sew (Fig. 8–17). For each side, stop at the corner and repeat the back-stitch, fold, and stitch process.

7. On the last side, stop 8"–10" from the end of the binding. Remove the quilt from the machine. Unfold the beginning end of the binding and cut it at a 45-degree angle. Refold the end (Fig. 8–18). Place it inside the tail end.

8. Mark the tail end where the edge of the miter starts (Fig. 8–19). Place a second mark on the tail end ½" from the first mark, toward the beginning end (Fig. 8–20).

9. Using the direction of the mitered end as a guide for the direction of the angle, cut the tail end at a 45-degree angle at the second mark.

10. With the binding ends unfolded and right sides together, join the ends with a ¼" seam allowance (Fig. 8–21). Trim the "dog ears" and press the seam allowances open.

11. Smooth the binding strip on the quilt and finish sewing the binding to the quilt across the joined ends.

12. Wrap the binding to the back and blind stitch it to the backing, following the visible stitching line (fig. 8–22).

Fig. 8–18. Cut the beginning end of the binding at a 45-degree angle.

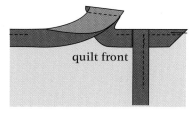

Fig. 8–21. Sew the ends together.

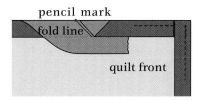

Fig. 8–19. Mark along the edge of the angled cut.

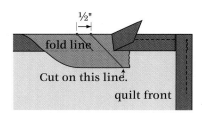

Fig. 8–20. Mark the tail end and ½" from the first mark.

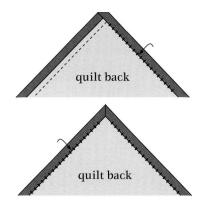

Fig. 8–22. Fold the binding over the raw edges and blind stitch.

Chapter 9

The Projects

Make an heirloom for today.

  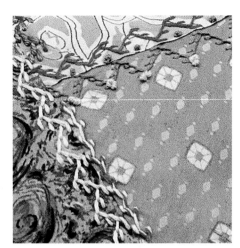

One of the many advantages of crazy stitching is its adaptability to an endless number of projects. In the next pages, you will find several projects requiring varied skill levels and time commitments. These projects are based on the multiple styles examined in the early chapters. Crazy stitching will embrace a budgeted schedule. Just remember to match the project to your proficiency and interest level. The most intense project is the patchwork quilt. The quickest is the greeting card. In between, you will find a pillow, vest, and sewing totes. From that point, I trust you'll take these ideas on your own and style your plans...your way.

Basic sewing necessities of sewing machine, utility, and decorative threads and general sewing tools (scissors, pins, etc.) are required for each item. Each project has general directions, easily adapted to your needs. Consider each idea, then expand or reduce the size, the embellishment, and the detail to your liking. If you need a quick and easy project, sew the small sewing kit or a pillow wrap. If you want a beautiful investment piece, sew a full-sized quilt or an embellished garment.

All of the projects are considered easy, but for your convenience, a skill level has been assigned to each one:

Beginner = for someone with little or no sewing experience.

Early intermediate = still easy for a beginner, but the project takes a little more time.

Intermediate = still easy but some sewing experience helpful; project requires more time.

Pillow Sleeve

The pillow sleeve is a crazy-patch tube, designed to fit around a favorite pillow. It is simple to construct, so you can consider making several to change the mood of a room or the style of a chair.

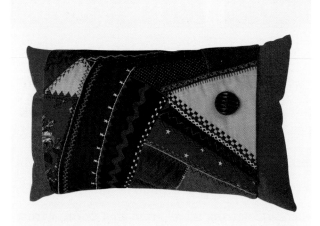

Supplies

Fabrics

The yardage is based on fabric at least 40" wide.

Patch scraps
Muslin foundation, ½ yard
Pillow sleeve lining, ½ yard
Purchased decorator knife-edged pillow

Notions

Utility and decorative threads
Embellishments

How-to

1. Use a tape measure to measure around the pillow at its center as shown in Figs. 9–1a and b. Measure the length of the pillow also.

• Cut a muslin foundation for the crazy patch, as follows:

sleeve length = the measurement around the pillow plus 4"

sleeve width = the length of the pillow less 2" (the sleeve will finish 1" narrower)

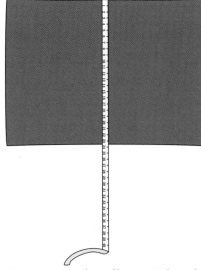

Fig. 9–1a. Measure the pillow's girth and length.

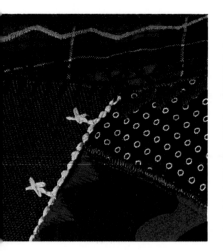  

2. Construct and embellish the crazy patch on the muslin foundation. Trim the length of the piece to the measurement around the pillow plus ½" for seam allowances. Trim the width as desired, allowing ½" for seam allowances. When trimming the width, think about how much of the pillow you want to show (1" to 4" on each side of the sleeve looks nice).

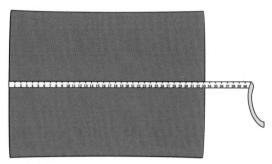

Fig. 9–1b.

3. Cut a pillow sleeve lining the same measurements as the trimmed crazy-patch piece. Place the crazy-patch piece and the lining right sides together and sew around the outside edge with a ¼" seam allowance, leaving one end partially unsewn for turning (Fig. 9–2).

leave unsewn →

Fig. 9–2. Sew the pieces right sides together.

4. Turn the piece right side out through the unsewn opening. Whip-stitch the opening closed.

5. Whip-stitch the short ends together, creating a tube (Fig. 9–3). Slide the sleeve over the pillow.

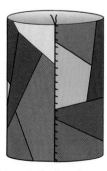

Fig. 9–3. Whip-stitch the short ends together.

Early intermediate

Pillow

It seems we never have enough pillows. They are attractive in almost every room, fit almost every chair, and lend themselves to a moderate sewing investment. This easily constructed pillow is based on the classic directions of straight-stitch appliqué and decorative machine embellishment.

Supplies

Fabrics
The yardage is based on fabric at least 40" wide.
- Patch scraps
- Muslin foundation, 14" square
- Lining, ½ yard
- Contrasting fabric for
    wrapping cord edging

NOTIONS
- Utility and decorative threads
- Cording equal to the pillow's perimeter
    plus 6" (about 55")
- 12" pillow form
- Buttons for back (optional)
- Embellishments

How-to

CRAZY PATCH
1. Following the instructions beginning on page 68, crazy-patch and embellish the 14" square. Trim the square to 13".

CORDING
2. Make straight-of-grain or bias strips. The strip width is equal to the diameter of the cord plus 1", and the length is equal to the pillow perimeter plus 6".
- Wrap the strip around the cording, right side out, aligning the long edges of the strip.
- With a zipper foot, cording foot, or edge-stitch foot, sew the fabric strip snugly around the cord (Fig. 9–4).

Fig. 9–4. Sew fabric strips around the cord.

- Sew the covered cord around the edges of the crazy-patch square. Overlap the cord ends. They will be caught in the seam when the front and back of the pillow are sewn together.

Fig. 9–5. Sew a facing to each back piece.

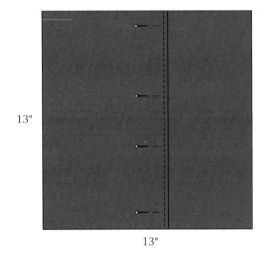

13"

13"

Fig. 9–6. Overlap the back pieces and baste.

PILLOW BACK

3. For a plain pillow back, cut a 13" square of fabric. Skip to Step 4.

• For a back with buttons, cut two pieces, each 8" x 13", and two facing pieces, 2½" x 13".

• Sew a facing piece, right sides together, to each back piece as shown in Fig. 9–5.

• Fold each facing to the back and press. Pin to hold them in place. Construct three button-holes in the faced side of the left back piece.

• Overlap the two faced edges of the back pieces to form a 13" square. Machine baste.

• Sew buttons on the plain side, matching the buttonholes.

JOIN FRONT AND BACK

4. Place the plain or buttoned pillow back on the crazy-patch square, right sides together (Fig. 9–6).

• Following the cording stitch line, sew the sandwich of front, cording, and back together.

• For the plain pillow back, be sure to leave the seam partially unsewn along one edge for turning the pillow cover right side out and inserting the pillow. For the buttoned back, sew all the way around the edge.

• Remove the basting stitches, turn the pillow right side out, insert the pillow form, and button the buttons.

Beginner

Greeting Card

One of my favorite "love gifts" is a personally embellished card. Card racks and card catalogs have blank greeting cards with the center cut-away, designed for a photo or special drawing. Use these cards for crazy-patch embellishment. Simply construct a small patch of "crazies" and insert your designed fabric behind the opening. Make a special gift, matched to the occasion.

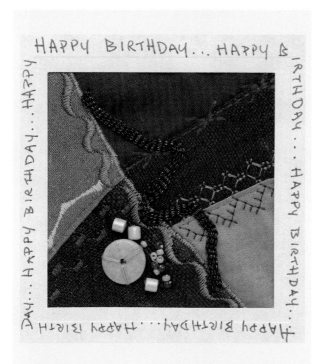

Greeting cards that are designed for fabric insertions have an extra paper sheet to fold and glue to the wrong side of the insertion. The sheet conceals all the "back work."

Trim the crazy-patch unit about ½" larger than the opening in the card. Using a fabric glue stick, adhere the crazy patch to the wrong side of the card opening, then glue the extra paper sheet over the back of the crazy patch.

Supplies

Fabrics
Patch scraps
Foundation fabric, 6" square

Notions
Utility and decorative threads
Frame-style greeting card
Glue stick
Colored markers (optional to add
    design detail to card)

Intermediate

Crazy-Patch Vest

A favorite accent garment, the vest begs for embellishment. This crazy-patch approach is so versatile that most wardrobes really need two vests, one heavily embellished and another in simple stitches more suited to the routine of your life. Select your best vest pattern and turn it into a crazy-stitch sensation.

Supplies

Fabrics

Patch scraps

Muslin foundation, refer to your pattern for yardage

Lining fabric, refer to your pattern for yardage

Bias binding, ½ yard

Notions

Vest pattern

Utility and decorative threads

Buttons, old laces, etc. (optional)

General sewing supplies

How-To

CRAZY PATCH

1. Cut muslin rectangles for the front and back of the vest. Trace the pattern shape onto each muslin piece with a permanent marking pen.

2. Crazy-patch and embellish each section, aligning the patch flow attractively across the center front.

Note: To maintain a uniform shape, crazy patch and embellish each rectangle *before* cutting vest.

VEST PATTERN

3. Place and pin the vest pattern pieces over the embellished crazy patch, aligning the pattern with the original marked lines on the muslin. Trim each vest unit to the exact pattern shape. Sew the vest together at the side and shoulder seams.

4. Cut and sew the lining with the same pattern. Press open the seam allowances of the lining and vest. Place the wrong side of vest to the wrong side of the lining, aligning the shoulder and side seams, center back, center front, arm hole. Pin or baste.

BUTTON LOOP

5. Use the pattern's suggested button closure or, for a custom look, make the following button loop.

• Cut a ½" x 12" bias strip to fold and stitch for a button closure loop.

• Fold the strip in half lengthwise right side out (Fig. 9–7). Press.

Fig. 9–7. Fold the strip in half.

• Open the center fold and fold the long edges to center, matching the fold line (Fig. 9–8). Press.

Fig. 9–8. Fold the long edges to the center.

• Refold on the center line and stitch along the edge to create a strip about ⅜" wide.

• Select a large, attractive button to complement your vest.

• To determine the finished loop length, place the button at the desired location on the vest front. Place one end of the bias strip at the edge of the other vest front. Loop the strip around the button. Pin in place. Cut the excess strip length away at the vest edge (Fig. 9–9). The loop ends will be covered by the binding.

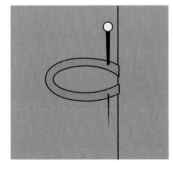

Fig. 9–9. Pin the loop to the right center front.

BINDING

6. Measure the linear distance around all the vest edges. Cut a continuous 2" bias strip equal to the linear distance plus 12". Fold the bias strip in half lengthwise, right side out, and press.

7. To apply the binding, start at the bottom of a side seam on the right side of the vest. Align the raw edges of the binding strip with the raw edges of the vest.

• Machine sew the bias binding to the vest with a ½" seam allowance. Roll the binding to the back and blind stitch to the lining.

8. Sew a button in place, aligning it with the button loop on the opposite side.

Early Intermediate

Sewing Caddy

Enjoy making a simple caddy, designed to hold scissors, pencils, etc. You will find it a convenient accessory to drop in a sewing tote for a guild workshop or for use with your favorite car projects. Try changing the dimensions to meet other tote needs. Construct them the same way. Just divide the pockets differently. This sewing caddy was inspired by one that belonged to one of my students.

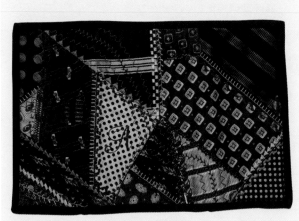

Caddy outside

Supplies

Fabrics

Muslin foundation, 12" x 18"
Patch scraps
Lining, 10½" x 16½"
Pockets, 10½" x 16½"

Notions

Low-loft batting, 12" x 18"
Utility and decorative thread
1 yard of ½"-wide grosgrain ribbon

How-To

CRAZY PATCH

1. Following the instructions beginning on page 68, crazy-patch and embellish the 12" x 18" muslin piece. Trim it to 10½" x 16½".

LINING

2. Use your favorite pattern to machine quilt the batting to the lining piece or tie the caddy as in the illustration below.

POCKETS

3. Fold the pocket piece in half lengthwise (Fig. 9–10).

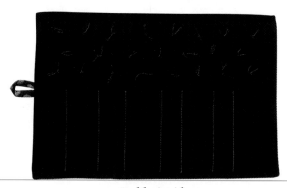

Caddy inside

• Lay the folded pocket piece on the lining side of the lining/batting piece. With a narrow satin stitch, sew through the pocket piece, lining, and batting to create pockets in widths to suit your needs (Fig. 9–11). Pull threads to the back and tie.

Fig. 9–10. Fold the pocket piece in half.

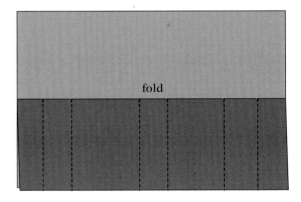

fold

Fig. 9–11. Create pockets of various widths.

FINISHING

4. Finish the sewing caddy by the pillow-slip or the bias-binding method.

Pillow-slip method

• For tying, sew a ribbon lengthwise down the center of the crazy-patch piece (Fig. 9–12) or complement with a button closure.
• Place the crazy-patch piece, right sides together, over the lining/pocket piece.
• Sew with a ¼" seam allowance around outer edge, leaving one end open for turning.
• Turn the caddy right side out and blind stitch the open end.

Bias-binding method

• Sew ribbon lengthwise down the center of the crazy-patch piece.
• Place the wrong sides of the crazy-patch and the lining/pocket pieces together.
• Pin together to hold the placement.
• Cut bias fabric strips 2½" wide by the length around caddy plus 8". Use the folded strip to bind the raw edges, as described on page 108.

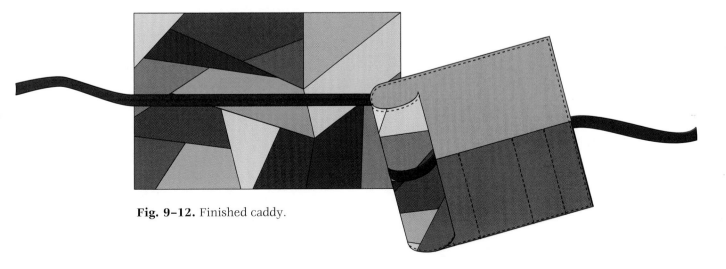

Fig. 9–12. Finished caddy.

Needle Tote

Often, we find it convenient to tuck a small sewing project in a travel bag. This carrier is perfect for a few pins, special needles, thread, and scissors.

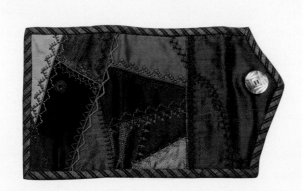

Supplies

Fabrics

Patch scraps

Muslin foundation, 6" x 11"

Decorator fabric for lining, 6" x 11"

Pocket, 6" x 6"

Bias binding for top of pocket

Notions

Snap closure (½" coat snaps are ideal)

Wonderful old button for decoration

Utility and decorative threads

Wool felt for needle holder

Templates

Tote

Pocket

How-to

TEMPLATES

1. From the full-sized pattern on page 127, make templates from paper, lightweight cardboard, or plastic for the tote and the pocket.

CRAZY PATCH

2. Following the instructions beginning on page 69, crazy-patch and embellish the muslin foundation.

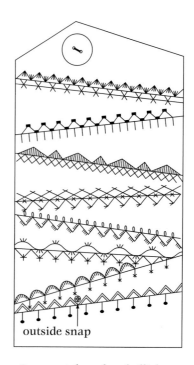

Crazy-patch and embellish

- Use the tote template to cut the crazy-patch piece to size. Templates include ¼" seam allowances.

3. Optional—add a light batting to the crazy-patch piece, if you like.

LINING

4. Also use the tote template to trace and cut a lining from the decorator fabric.

5. Use the pocket template to trace and cut a pocket.

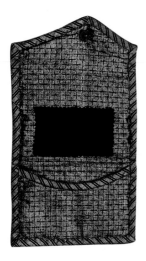

- Cover the top edge of the pocket with a length of bias binding.

- With both pieces right side up, pin the pocket to the lining (Fig. 9–13).

6. Use pinking shears to cut a small rectangle of wool felt for the needle holder.

- Sew down the center of the felt rectangle to attach it to the right side of the lining (Fig. 9–14).

TOTE ASSEMBLY

7. Place the crazy-patch and lining pieces right sides together. Sew around the outside edge with a ¼" seam allowance, leaving an opening for turning.

- Trim the extra seam allowance material from the corners and turn the piece right side out. Press lightly.

- Sew the button on the tote front and the snap underneath the button (Fig. 9–15). Sew the second part of the snap on the crazy-patch side so the tote will close easily.

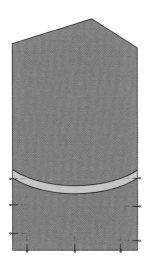

Fig. 9–13. Pin the pocket to the lining.

Fig. 9–14. Sew the wool felt rectangle to the lining.

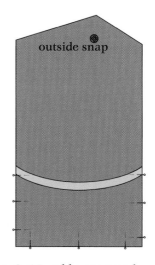

Fig. 9–15. Add a snap under the button.

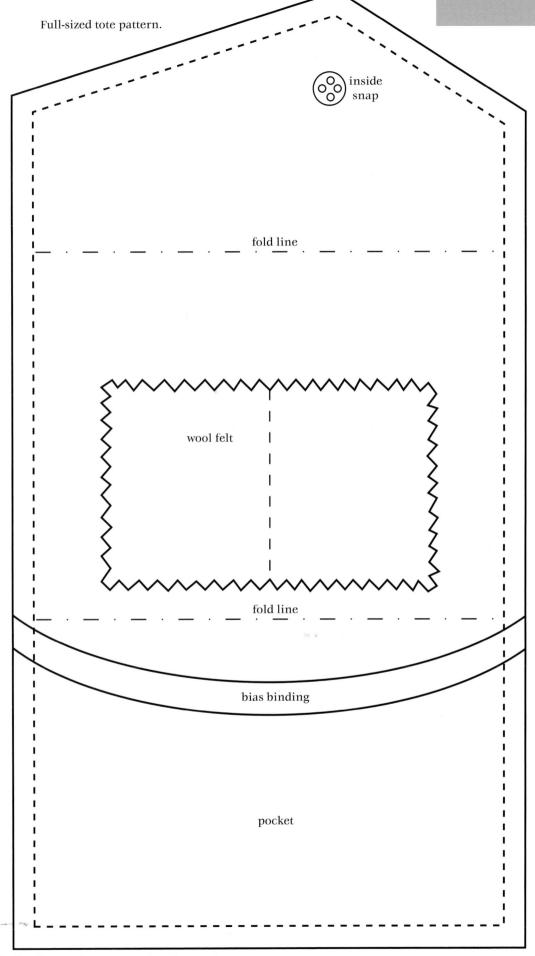

Full-sized tote pattern.

inside snap

fold line

wool felt

fold line

bias binding

pocket

Intermediate

Appliqué Patchwork Quilt

Crazy patch can be integrated with other techniques. The random patches and decorative embellishments look great with appliqué and simple patchwork units. This quilt is made of 12" blocks containing simple appliqué, four-patch, and crazy-patch units. If you want the quilt to be larger or you would like to change the energy of the quilt, insert one or two sashing strips in each row. Arrange the same number of sashing strips in each row. The backing and border yardage and the cut lengths of the border strips will allow for the insertions.

SEW CRAZY 78" X 90"
Block 12"

Supplies

Notions

Fusible web for appliqué, if desired
   24" wide x 2 yards
Utility and decorative threads
Low-loft batt, 82" x 94"

Fabrics

The yardage is based on fabric at least 40" wide.

Crazy patch unit, 30 – 6½" squares
   Assorted fabrics to blend with the crazy patch, total 2½ yards
   Muslin foundation, 1½ yards
Four-patch unit, 30 – 6½" squares
   Assorted linens in coordinated colors, total 2¾ yards
Random sashing insets (optional),
   ⅓ yard
Appliqué unit, 30 – 6½" x 12½" rectangles

   BACKGROUNDS, assorted linens in co-ordinated colors, total 2½ yards
   FLOWERS, assorted linens in colors from the patchwork, total 1 yard
   STEMS, ⅓ yard

Inner border, 2¾ yards
Outer border, 2¾ yards
Backing, 5½ yards
Binding, 1 yard

How-To

CRAZY-PATCH UNITS

1. Cut 30 muslin squares 7".
- Crazy-patch and straight-stitch appliqué each square.
- Embellish the squares with embroidery.
- Trim each square to 6½".

FOUR-PATCH UNITS

2. Cut the linen fabrics in strips 3½" x 14".
- Sew a light and a dark strip, right sides together, with a ¼" seam allowance. Sew a variety of these strip sets.
- Cross-cut each strip set into four 3½" sections (Fig. 9–16). You will need a total of 60 sections.

Fig. 9–16. Cut strip sets into 3½" sections.

- Sew two sections of mixed colors together to make a four-patch (Fig. 9–17). Make 30 four-patch units.

Fig. 9–17. Four-patch unit.

APPLIQUÉ UNITS

3. Trace and cut templates for the flowers and stems from the full-sized patterns on pages 132 and 133.
- Use the templates to cut the pieces for 34 flowers and 34 stems.
- Cut 30 rectangles 7" x 13" from the background fabrics.
- Appliqué the 30 flowers and stems.
- Trim the units to 6½" x 12½".

QUILT ASSEMBLY

4. Arrange the crazy-patch, four-patch, and appliqué units to form blocks (Fig. 9–18). Sew the units together to make 30 blocks.

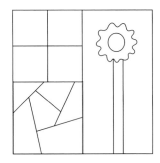

Fig. 9–18. Block assembly.

- Arrange the blocks in 6 rows of 5 blocks each. The blocks can be turned in any direction (Fig. 9–19).
- Add two random sashing inserts per row, if desired. You will need (12) 1½" x 12½" strips (Fig. 9–20).
- Sew the blocks together in rows, then join the rows. Press as you go.
- Press and square the quilt top.

INSERTION STRIP

5. Follow the directions on page 104 to apply a contrasting insertion strip around the quilt edge, if desired.

Fig. 9–19. Quilt assembly without sashing.

BORDERS

6. In the quilt in the photo, the border strips vary in width. The pattern instructions, however, call for a uniform border 9" wide.

Inner border:
• Cut four strips 9½" wide, parallel to the selvages.

Outer border:
• Cut four fabric strips 4½" wide, parallel to the selvages.
• Cut four 4½"-wide strips down the length of the fusible web.
• Fuse the web strips to the outer border strips.
• Cut random curves along one edge of each fused outer border strip.

Border assembly:
• Fuse the curved border strips to the inner border strips. The combined width should be 9½" (Fig. 9–21).

Fig. 9–20. Quilt assembly with sashing.

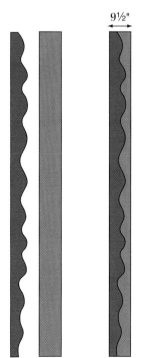

9½"

HINT
• *Use an opened file folder to draw a template for the random curve.*

Fig. 9–21. Fuse the outer border strip to the inner border strip.

- Edge-stitch appliqué the curved edges.
- Sew the border strips to the quilt and miter the corners.
- Appliqué stems and flowers to the corners.

FINISHING

7. Cut the backing yardage in half crosswise to make two panels. Cut one panel in half lengthwise, then sew the three lengths together (minus selvages) as shown in Fig. 9–22. Press seam allowances open.

- Layer the backing, batting if used, and quilt top. Baste.
- Quilt or tie the layers.
- Bind the raw edges of the quilt with the double-fold, straight-grain binding (described on pages 108 and 109).

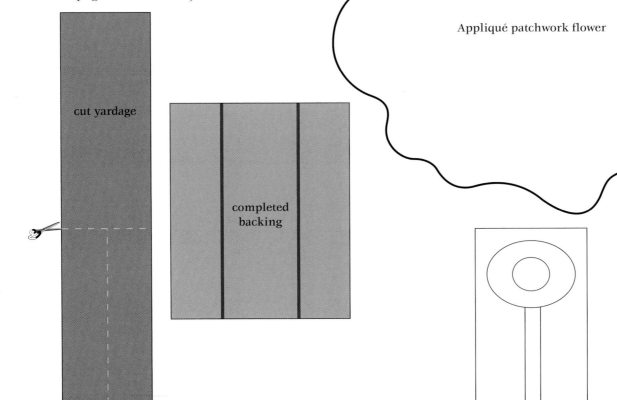

Flower center

Flower center

Appliqué patchwork flower

Fig. 9–22. Join the three backing pieces.

cut yardage

completed backing

Appliqué placement

Full-sized appliqué patterns.

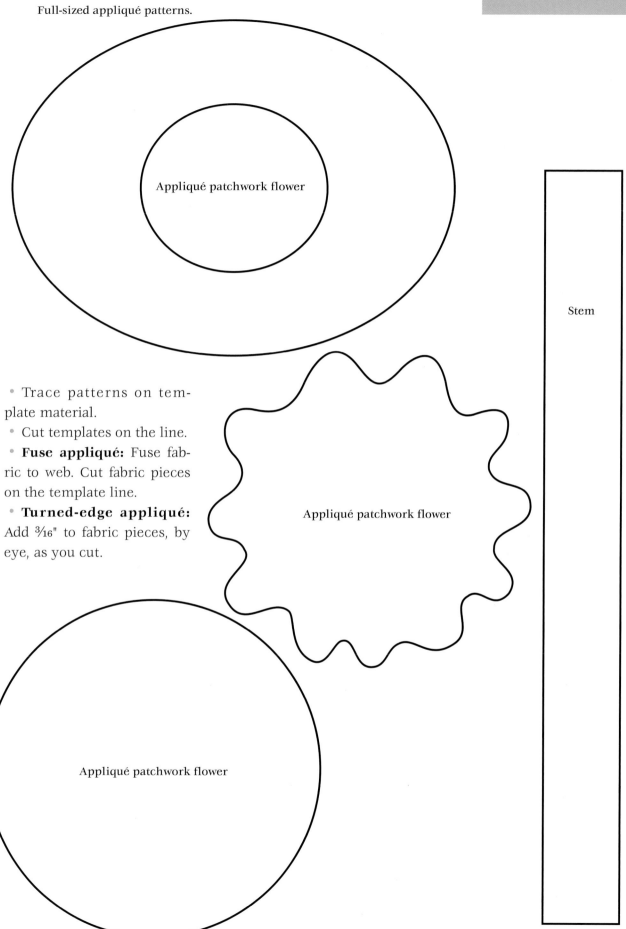

Appliqué patchwork flower

Stem

• Trace patterns on template material.
• Cut templates on the line.
• **Fuse appliqué:** Fuse fabric to web. Cut fabric pieces on the template line.
• **Turned-edge appliqué:** Add $\frac{3}{16}$" to fabric pieces, by eye, as you cut.

Appliqué patchwork flower

Appliqué patchwork flower

Guest Quilters

One of the pleasures of sharing needlework in guilds, workshops and such is the discovery of another's skill and approach to a topic. I asked a group of talented women to share their style in a sample piece of crazy quilt. Each artist is a talent in her own right. Some of my friends are professionals. Others enjoy stitchery as an accent to their lives. Their work is featured here and throughout the book. Enjoy the show.

Rainbow Riff

48" x 63", made by Dixie Haywood, Pensacola, Florida.

Dixie enjoys creating an understated embellishment on her crazy quilts. Her interest is in the interaction between the graphics of a design and the texture of the created fabric.

Alice Kolb – Sew Crazy with Decorative Threads & Stitches

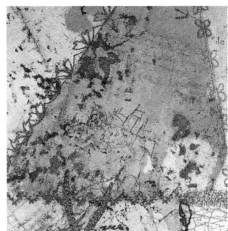

Nature's Images Series III – Daylilies

23" x 26½", made by Judy Simmons, Marietta, Georgia.

DAYLILIES is a composite of Judy's skill in fabric dying, designing, and stitching. It is one of a series of designs focused on the garden theme. Judy approached the daylily in a close-up profile of detail complimented by a tone-on-tone crazy-patch background.

Linen Scraps

25" x 25", made by Mary Honeycutt, Somerville, Alabama.

Mary designed the quilt from a collection of favorite linens. Taking an interesting approach to the obvious crazy style, Mary zigzagged and satin-stitch embellished all the units in a neutral thread, then complimented her stitching with a matching border.

All That Jazz

16" x 19", made by Fran Patterson, Austin, Texas.

ALL THAT JAZZ is a watercolor painted, fabric overlay appliqué, accented with a crazy pieced frame. A fiber-collage artist, Fran thrives on using textiles in an unpredictable way.

Crazy for QBL

24" x 29", made by Jan
Moore, Wilmington,
Delaware.

Jan designed and stitched
her crazy quilt in the traditional Victorian style from
her stash of velvets, satins,
and silks. She complemented each patch with charms
and trims that hold personal
meaning.

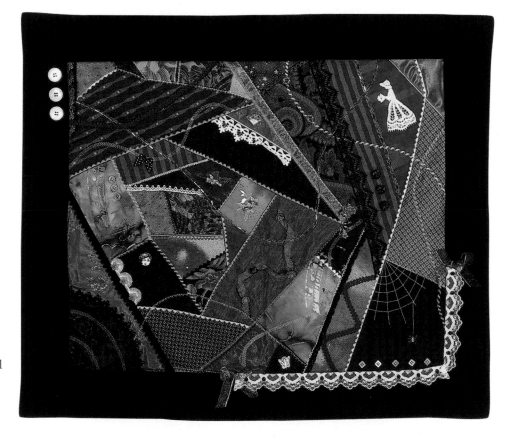

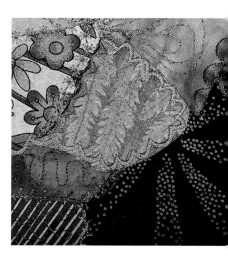

New Zealand Revisited

18" x 31", made by Mary
Lou Schwinn, Cazenovia,
New York.

Working in a variety of fabrics collected on her New
Zealand travels, Mary Lou
designed her quilt in stylized geographic imagery. A
variety of rayon and cotton
threads sewn in machine
decorative stitches connect
the individualized pieces.

Snowflake Memories

40½" x 40½", made by
Pamella Gray, North Prairie,
Wisconsin.

Pam and her daughter, Jennifer Gray McCormick, created this crazy quilt as a result of an Amy Grant Christmas concert that evoked wonderful memories of family times together.

Resources

BOOKS

Bond, Dorothy. *Crazy Quilting Stitches*. Cottage Grove, Oregon, 1981.

Dobbs, Christine. *Crazy Quilting*. Nashville: Rutledge Hill Press, 1998.

Enthoven, Jacqueline. *The Stitches of Creative Embroidery*. New York: Van Nostrand Reinhold Co., 1964.

Haigh, Janet. *Crazy Patchwork*. Chicago: The Quilt Digest Press, 1998.

Hall, Jane, and Dixie Haywood. *Foundation Quilts*. Paducah, Kentucky: American Quilter's Society, 2000.

Holmes, Val. *The Machine Embroiderer's Workbook*. London: BT Batsford Ltd., 1991.

Howard, Constance. *The Constance Howard Book of Stitches*. London: BT Batsford Ltd., 1979.

Jenkins, Susan, and Linda Seward. *The American Quilt Story*. Emmaus, Pennsylvania: Rodale Press. 1991

Kile, Michael. *The Quilt Digest*. San Francisco: The Quilt Digest Press, 1985.

Kolb, Alice Allen. *Sashiko by Machine*. Aurora, Illinois: Bernina of America, Inc., 1992.

    Crazy Patch by Machine. Aurora, Illinois: Bernina of America, Inc., 1997.

Lang, Donna, and Lucretia Robertson. *Decorating with Fabric*. New York: Clarkson N. Potter, Inc., 1986.

McMorris, Penny. *Crazy Quilts*. New York: EP Dutton, 1984.

Michler, J. Marsha. *The Magic of Crazy Quilting*. Iola, Wisconsin: Krause Publications, 1998.

    Crazy Quilts by Machine. Iola, Wisconsin: Krause Publications, 2000.

Montano, Judith. *The Crazy Quilt Handbook*. Lafayette, California: C&T Publishing, 1986.

    Crazy Quilt Odyssey. Martinez, California: C&T Publishing, 1991.

Potter, Meryl. *Crazy Patchwork*. Port Melbourne, Victoria: Thomas C. Lothian Pty. Ltd., 1998.

Samples, Carol. *Treasury of Crazyquilt Stitches*. Paducah, Kentucky: American Quilter's Society, 1999.

Wagner, Debra. *Traditional Quilts, Today's Techniques*. Iola, Wisconsin: Krause Publications, 1997.

Warren, Elizabeth, and Sharon L. Eisenstat. *Glorious American Quilts*. New York: Penguin Studio, Museum of American Folk Art, 1996.

MAGAZINES

American Quilter
American Patchwork and Quilting
Ornament
Quilter's Newsletter Magazine

WEB SITES

about.com – (search crazy quilt)

kirkcollection.com – (Antique quilts, antique & reproduction fabrics, crazy quilting)

geocities.com/SoHo/Lofts/6531 – (Crazy Quilt Central)

About the Author

From a discovery of quiltmaking in the 1970s to her current endeavors in teaching, writing, and designing, Alice has maintained a strong connection to the quilt world. With a masters degree in home economics, Alice's professional life began in the college classroom, where she taught clothing construction, textiles, and related subjects. Alice has taught quiltmaking throughout the United States, Japan, and Switzerland. From 1985 to 1994, she taught and designed for a major sewing machine exporter. She also taught at various conferences and guilds. Enjoying the "stretch of the sewing machine," she developed easy machine techniques for sashiko, decorative machine embellishment, and crazy quilting. Designing and teaching simple piecing and embellishment on understated wearables and quilts became her trademark.

Alice has worked as a regular contributor to various publications, having written articles for *Threads, American Quilter, Traditional Quilter,* and *Creative Needle.* She has also written numerous educational pamphlets and two books, *Sashiko Made Simple* and *Crazy Quilt by Machine* for Bernina. In 2000, Alice was honored by *Threads* magazine as one of three invitational participants in the 2000 Design Challenge. She has judged the American Quilter's Fashion Show several times and twice participated in the Fairfield Fashion show.

Making her home in the Texas Hill Country, Alice spends her free time with family and friends and enjoys her flower gardens and goats.

Other AQS Books

This is only a small selection of the books available from the American Quilter's Society. AQS books are known worldwide for timely topics, clear writing, beautiful color photos, and accurate illustrations and patterns. The following books are available from your local bookseller, quilt shop, or public library.

#6002   US$15.95

#5756   US$19.95

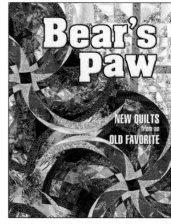

#5754   US$19.95

#5705   US$22.95

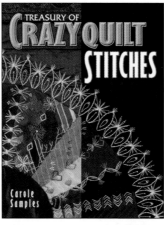

#5297   US$26.95

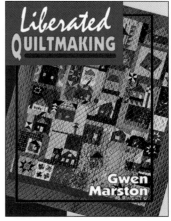

#4751   US$24.95

#5755   US$21.95

#5709   US$22.95

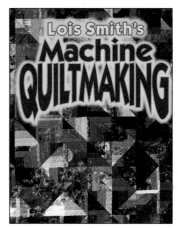

#4897   US$19.95

Look for these books nationally or call 1-800-626-5420